WEEKEND
DECORATING
PROJECTS

Better Homes and Gardens® Books
Des Moines, Iowa

Better Homes and Gardens® Books
An imprint of Meredith® Books

Better Homes and Gardens® Weekend Decorating Projects
Editor: Vicki L. Ingham
Contributing Editor: Jilann Severson
Art Director: Jerry J. Rank
Copy Chief: Catherine Hamrick
Copy and Production Editor: Terri Fredrickson
Contributing Copy Editor: Kathy Dorff
Contributing Proofreaders: Kathleen Richardson, Debra Morris Smith, Margaret Smith
Indexer: Sharon Duffy
Electronic Production Coordinator: Paula Forest
Editorial and Design Assistants: Kaye Chabot, Judy Bailey, Treesa Landry, Karen Schirm
Production Director: Douglas M. Johnston
Production Manager: Pam Kvitne
Assistant Prepress Manager: Marjorie J. Schenkelberg

Meredith® Books
Editor in Chief: James D. Blume
Design Director: Matt Strelecki
Managing Editor: Gregory H. Kayko
Executive Shelter Editor: Denise L. Caringer

Director, Sales & Marketing, Retail: Michael A. Peterson
Director, Sales & Marketing, Special Markets: Rita McMullen
Director, Sales & Marketing, Home & Garden Center Channel: Ray Wolf
Director, Operations: George A. Susral

Vice President, General Manager: Jamie L. Martin

Better Homes and Gardens® **Magazine**
Editor in Chief: Jean LemMon
Executive Interior Design Editor: Sandra S. Soria

Meredith Publishing Group
President, Publishing Group: Christopher M. Little
Vice President, Consumer Marketing & Development: Hal Oringer

Meredith Corporation
Chairman and Chief Executive Officer: William T. Kerr

Chairman of the Executive Committee: E. T. Meredith III

Cover Photograph: King Au. Instructions for the project shown are on *pages 48–49*.

All of us at Better Homes and Gardens® Books are dedicated to providing you with information and ideas to enhance your home. We welcome your comments and suggestions. Write to us at: Better Homes and Gardens® Books, Shelter Editorial Department, 1716 Locust St., Des Moines, IA 50309-3023.

If you would like to purchase additional copies of any of our books, check with your local bookstore.

WEEKEND
DECORATING
PROJECTS
CONTENTS

IF YOUR PASSION FOR PEACH HAS BEEN replaced by a yearning for yellow and all of your rooms seem tired and boring, it's time for a change. But you don't have to throw out all of your furniture and start over. Breathe new life into rooms without spending a lot of time and money by choosing projects that have a big impact on the way the room feels. Window and wall treatments, floor coverings, furniture, and decorative accessories all help shape the mood and style of a room, and altering any one of them can energize the setting. Transform more than one of them, and before you know it, you'll have created a whole new look.

THE MAGIC OF MAKEOVERS

Tidy up clutter with a new chest of drawers made by stacking two similar units. For details that make a difference, glue fringe to a plain shelf or crown a candle with a handmade shade. And give your chairs a fresh new look with slipcovers.

How to decide where to start? Think about the mood you'd like to evoke. If a room that used to feel warm and cozy now seems dark and heavy, lighten the look by dressing a couple of armchairs in simple slipcovers. Choose crisp, clear pastels and keep patterns to a minimum for a fresh, uncluttered feeling. Add new purchased pillows or slipcover your old ones; replace an oriental-style wool rug with a woven cotton one. Pay attention to details, too—an edging of fringe or Victorian millwork on a shelf adds a note of whimsy that perks up a room's personality.

If, on the other hand, the neutrals you once found serene now seem cold and bland, jazz up your rooms with bold color and pattern. Lay the foundation with a painted canvas floorcloth, then pick up the colors with new shades or valances at the windows. Emphasize the scheme (and add panache) by covering a plain lamp shade with coordinating paper or fabric.

Another easy way to give your room a makeover is to create a fresh focal point—an object or an area that catches your attention and draws you into the room. Often it's a fireplace or bank of windows, but a new piece of handpainted furniture located in a prominent position can do the trick, too. Or reconsider the possibilities of an architectural feature like the windows shown here. A cushion and pillows turn the recess into a comfy seat; a simple swag-and-jabot valance frames the view.

In this book, you'll find a wide variety of weekend projects to build, paint, or sew. Choose any one of them—or several—to invigorate your rooms. You'll be amazed what a difference a day or two can make!

Thanks to the magic of a makeover, a pair of deeply set windows flanked by bookcases (left case not shown) becomes a cozy nook for reading, conversation, or daydreaming. A simple swag-and-jabot valance softens the window (see page 14 for instsructions). Purchased blinds installed behind the valance provide

BEFORE

privacy at night. A gussetted cushion in fabric to match the valance turns the deep sill into a comfortable seat (see page 87 for instructions). Add layers of plump pillows—the long, ruffled one is a variation of the piped and ruffled cushion on page 88. Draw up a table and chairs to complete the transformation.

IMAGINE YOURSELF INSIDE A BOX. Cut some openings to let in the light, and you have a basic room—windows, walls, and floors. How can you give that box some instant personality?

Paint and wallpaper may be the first things that come to mind for walls, but they're not the only solutions. Add visual interest by decoupaging walls with prints, adding a chair rail, or hanging fabric.

Because so many options for dressing windows are available, we've chosen a few that

WINDOWS
WALLS & FLOORS

are especially easy or offer creative solutions to privacy problems. Many of these treatments take so little time to install that you can change them on a whim.

Finally, don't underestimate the power of what's underfoot to change a room. A colorful painted rug or a stenciled canvas floorcloth can brighten a dark, dull room, introduce a new color scheme, or emphasize a favorite motif drawn from pillows or draperies.

If you're tired of plain walls, decoupage botanical prints directly onto them. You don't have to do a whole room with stenciled borders like the one opposite— that would take more than one weekend—but even one wall will have a big impact.

1. FABRIC BANNER

If you can sew a straight seam, you can make this fabric banner. Hung above lace café curtains, it affords privacy and adds color and softness. Use the same fabric on both sides, or make it reversible for two different looks.

1. MATERIALS

*Fabric and lining (see measuring
   instructions)*
Thread to match fabric
Wooden drapery rings
Wooden or ceramic knobs

TOOLS

*Awl or drill
   (for installing knobs)*

INSTRUCTIONS

1 **To determine banner depth,** measure area you want banner to cover. (As a general rule, this type of valance should cover ⅔ to ¾ of window top.) For width, measure width of window(s). Multiply by 1⅓ for moderate swags and by 1½ for deeper swags. Add desired length for tails; add ½-inch seam allowances.

2 **Cut and piece fabric** as necessary to form 1 long panel each from fabric and lining. Stitch panels together, right sides facing, leaving an opening for turning. Turn, press, and slip-stitch opening closed.

3 **Allowing for length of tails,** divide banner width by number of windows. Use resulting figure to estimate positions of drapery rings. Check drape of swags by taping to

1. FABRIC BANNER

window frame; adjust as necessary, then handsew rings at marked points along top edge. Make pilot hole for each knob with awl or drill. Attach knobs. Hang rings from knobs.

2. TEA TOWELS

Who says fast and easy can't be clever, too? Have some fun with window treatments in the kitchen or bath—use cotton tea towels to replicate the look of Grandma's clothesline. Wooden drawer pulls hold the clothesline at the desired height.

2. MATERIALS

Tea towels
Clothesline rope to fit window
Wooden clothespins
Wooden drawer pulls

TOOLS

Awl or drill

INSTRUCTIONS

1 **Using awl or drill to make pilot holes,** install drawer pulls at desired height so tea towels will fall to desired depth. Rope will sag in center, making

WINDOW TREATMENTS

2. TEA TOWELS

3. TABLECLOTH

tea towels hang lower at that point.

2 **Tie rope to drawer pulls.** Pin towels to rope with clothespins.

DESIGNTIP ■ To create the effect of a flounce or valance, add lace kerchiefs along the top. Pinch each one at the center and secure it with the same clothespin that's holding the towel.

3. TABLECLOTH

For a quick change of mood or a temporary window dressing, drape a colorful vintage or lace tablecloth in the window. It couldn't be any easier—a tension rod is the trick. Since this treat-

ment doesn't affect the woodwork, it's ideal for apartments. Sunlight will fade fabrics, however, so only use those of little monetary or sentimental value.

3. MATERIALS
Vintage tablecloth
Tension rod to fit inside window frame

INSTRUCTIONS

1 **Fold tablecloth in half diagonally.** A square, round, or oval tablecloth will yield a symmetrical curtain. A

rectangular tablecloth will have an off-center point or jabots or tails of different lengths.

2 **Center rod along fold of tablecloth** and roll tablecloth around rod once. Place rod in window, adjusting and smoothing curtain as needed. Tablecloth should be pinched between rod and window frame on each side to secure.

TECHNIQUETIP ■ If half of the tablecloth is damaged, cut it in half diagonally and hem, then roll the hemmed edge around the rod and hang as described above.

1. FABRIC SHADE

Enjoy privacy while still admitting light with a shade that's sheer at the top and opaque at the bottom. To raise the shade, roll it up from the bottom and secure it at the desired height with ribbon ties.

1. MATERIALS
Sheer and opaque fabrics (for
yardages, see instructions)
Thread to match fabrics
1-inch-wide ribbon to measure
4 times height of window
1×2 pine board
L brackets and screws

TOOLS
Staple gun and staples
Scissors

1. FABRIC SHADE

INSTRUCTIONS

1 **Measure window** to determine fabric yardage: Opaque fabric will cover ⅔ of window for first-floor rooms and ½ for upper-story rooms; sheer fabric will cover remainder. Cut fabrics to required depths plus ⅝ inch for seam allowance; for width, add 1⅝ inch to window width for hems and returns (where fabric wraps board at top).

2 **Join fabric panels** with a flat-fell seam: Stitch pieces, wrong sides facing, with ⅝-inch seam allowance. Press seam open, then press both seam allowances toward opaque fabric. Trim sheer fabric seam allowance to ⅛ inch. Turn under opaque seam allowance ¼ inch and press over

seam, encasing sheer seam allowance. Topstitch along folded edge of opaque seam allowance.

3 **Hem sides.** Staple shade to pine board. Cut ribbon in half. Center and staple halves to board. Mount inside window frame (see *page 14*).

2. PAPER LACE SHADE

This no-sew window treatment filters light and screens unwanted views while adding a casual feeling to your interiors. The soft, pliable paper resembles nonwoven interfacing.

2. MATERIALS
Paper lace (available at art
supply stores)
Wire for hanging paper
2 screw eyes
Wooden clothespins

TOOLS
Scissors
Needle-nose pliers

INSTRUCTIONS

1 **Insert screw eye** in each side of window frame at desired height.

2. PAPER LACE SHADE

3. PAINTED PANES

Loop wire through one screw eye and twist on itself to secure. Using pliers, pull wire through other screw eye; stretch tightly and twist on itself.

2 **Cut paper to desired** depth and approximately 1½ times the width of the window. Attach paper to wire with clothespins at ends and middle. Gently pleat remaining paper and pin to wire.

3. PAINTED PANES

Enjoy lacy patterns of sunlight on your windowsill by stenciling the windowpanes with enamel paint and

paper doilies. Clean the windows with a mild soap-and-water solution. When you tire of the look, scrape off the paint with a razor blade.

3. MATERIALS

Paper doilies or commercial stencil
*   *adapted to fit window*
Spray stencil adhesive
*   *(not spray glue)*
Oil-based enamel paint
Stencil brush
Cellulose sponge
Ammonia

INSTRUCTIONS

1 **Clean windowpanes with ammonia.** (Commercial cleaners may leave residue.) Spray doily or stencil with stencil adhesive and adhere to window according to manufacturer's instructions. Paint window using a stencil brush and a tapping motion. Leave stencil in place and let paint dry overnight. Use cellulose sponge to apply a second coat of paint. Let dry, then remove stencil.

WINDOW SWAG & JABOT TREATMENT

This swag-and-jabot softens and frames a window with classic formality. It consists of three pieces: a draped swag and two pleated sides—the jabots or tails. If you don't want to make your own patterns, check fabric stores for patterns, which are available in several styles. The jabots shown on *page 15* are self-lined so the same fabric shows on both sides of the pleats. To play up the waterfall effect, line the jabots with contrasting fabrics. (Turn to *page 7* to see how this window treatment finishes off a window seat.)

INSTRUCTIONS

1 **To determine yardage,** use sheet to make patterns for swag and tails, then measure patterns. It may be easier to mock up patterns with valance shelf temporarily installed (see Step 7). Double the yardage for self-lining.

2 **To make swag pattern,** measure width of window and add about 8 inches. Determine desired depth of swag (usually 15 to 20 inches at center). Cut sheet to this size.

3 **Secure top edge of swag** to top of valance shelf with thumb tacks or push pins. Fold sheet in pleats at each end of shelf, allowing center of swag to drape to desired depth. Pin pleats; trim excess fabric and trim lower edge of swag in a curve. Mark swag's

MATERIALS

Old sheet for pattern
Fabric (for yardage
  requirements, see
  instructions)
Thread to match fabric
1×2 pine board
Two ³/₄-inch L brackets
4 screws

TOOLS

Staple gun and staples
Drill and screwdriver bit
  for drill

center point and pleats. Open out pleats; fold pattern in half to make sure pleats are even and adjust as necessary. Cutting line along side edges will zigzag, following pleat lines. Using pattern as a guide, cut out swag from fabric and lining, adding ½-inch seam allowances all around.

4 **To make pattern for jabots,** measure desired length for outside point (usually one-half to two-thirds the window length). Cut a 45-inch-wide piece of sheet to this length. Mark length of first, shortest pleat (usually about the depth of swag) on one edge; cut sheet on diagonal from that point to lower corner on opposite side (bottom of outside pleat). Starting with short edge, fold sheet in pleats to achieve effect shown on *page 15*. If valance will be hung outside window frame, allow 4 inches at

outside edge for return. Mark pleats and line where sheet folds over front edge of valance.

5 **Using pattern as guide** and allowing ½-inch seam allowances all around, cut 1 tail from fabric and lining. Reverse tail pattern to make second piece.

6 **With right sides facing,** stitch each pair of pieces together, leaving top edges open for turning. Turn and press. Pleat swag and tails according to patterns and baste across top edges to hold in place.

7 **Center and staple** raw edge of swag to 1 wide side of 1×2 board. Staple 1 jabot over each end (see photo, *below left*). If valance will be hung outside window frame, wrap outside edges of jabot around end of board as shown. If valance will be hung within window frame, align edge of jabot with edge of board.

8 **Fold fabric out of way.** Place board against window frame with stapled side up. Mark placement of L brackets (see photo, *below right*). Remove board and attach L bracket to each end of board. Reposition and screw L brackets to window.

Center swag on one side of 1x2 board and staple in place (this will be top). Starting at outside edge, staple jabot over swag.

Attach L brackets to both board and window frame to hold valance in place.

■ SHEER CURTAINS

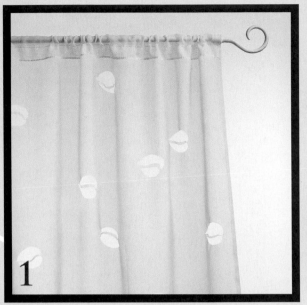

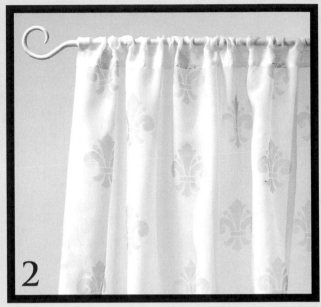

1. LEAF SILHOUETTES

A stencil-cutting tool that cuts plastic stencils with heat works well on sheer polyester curtains. The hot tip melts the edge of the fabric, leaving a clean, unfrayed line.

INSTRUCTIONS

1 **Enlarge leaf design,** *below,* **200 percent** and trace onto paper with black marker. Tape to work surface. Tape glass over pattern. Place rolled masking tape (sticky side out) around sides of glass.

2 **Press curtain.** Use pencil to mark placement of leaves with Xs. Press curtain on glass with an X over leaf pattern so fabric is taut. *Note: Stencil burner tip and shaft get very hot.* Keep tool moving quickly and smoothly and never touch tip. If melted residue collects on tip, carefully wipe on paper.

3 **To cut out design,** trace tip of stencil burner around edges of shape. Discard cutout sections.

1. MATERIALS
100 percent polyester sheer curtain
8×10-inch piece of glass

TOOLS
Masking tape or painters' tape
Pencil
Paper
Black marker
Electric stencil burner

2. STAMPED FLEUR-DE-LIS

Fabric stamping is easy with special, deeply cut stamps that are readily available at crafts stores. Just paint the surface and press the stamp to the curtain.

INSTRUCTIONS

1 **Prewash curtain** and dry without fabric softener. Press. Tape kraft paper to work surface. Tape curtain over paper. Using a pencil, mark desired placement of fleur-de-lis with a small X.

2 **Practice stamping** on scrap fabric similar to curtain or in an inconspicuous spot. Shake or stir paint well, then squirt onto paper plate. Brush a very light coat of paint onto the stamp, using applicator. Lightly press stamp to cloth, taking care not to move or rock it. Lift stamp away and repeat for additional designs. Let paint dry for 1 week; heat-set according to paint directions.

DESIGNTIP ■ See *page 21* for how to use the same technique to stamp your walls with a coordinating chair rail.

2. MATERIALS
Sheer curtain, preferably 100 percent cotton or cotton blend
Fleur-de-lis-shaped fabric and wall stamp
Stamping paint in 14K gold color

TOOLS
Kraft paper
Pencil
Artists' tape
Paper plate
Applicator sponges or paintbrushes for applying paint to stamp

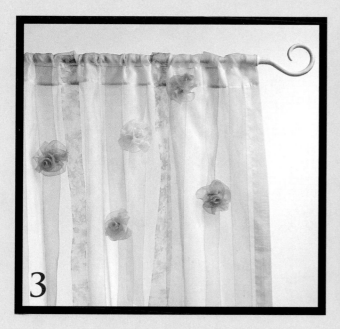

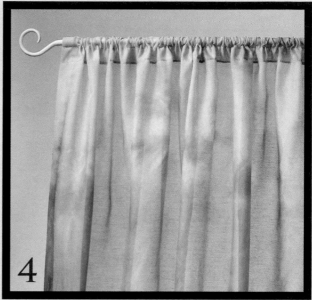

3. RIBBONS AND ROSES

For a decidedly feminine touch, dress up plain sheers with streamers of organdy ribbons dotted with ribbon roses.

INSTRUCTIONS

1 **Fold 1 end of each ribbon streamer** over curtain sleeve; stitch in place along casing line. Evenly space ribbons, depending on how tightly shirred curtain will be. Trim to desired lengths.

2 **To make ribbon rose,** knot ribbon 1 inch from 1 end. Loosely roll knotted end of tail clockwise several turns. Handstitch to secure. Fold ribbon back on itself and continue rolling clockwise several more turns. Handstitch to secure. Repeat folding and rolling once more. Sit rose on buckram base like a cup on a saucer and stitch in place. Gather bottom edge of ribbon, winding thread around base. Stitch to buckram. Trim ribbon tail and excess buckram. Pin or stitch roses to streamers as desired.

> #### 3. MATERIALS
> *Sheer curtain*
> *Organdy ribbon (1 floral and 4 solid colors) in the following amounts:*
>   *¾ yard of 1½-inch-wide ribbon for each streamer*
>   *1 yard of 1½-inch-wide ribbon for each rose*
> *2×2-inch scrap of buckram for base of each rose*
> *Thread to match curtain*
> #### TOOLS
> *Sewing needle*

4. CUSTOM-DYED SHEERS

Dye sheers to match your walls or furniture. The shaded effect produces a fool-the-eye look of filtered sunlight.

INSTRUCTIONS

1 **Cover large work area with newspaper,** then with plastic. Wash curtain without fabric softener. Spread wet curtain onto plastic. Finger-pleat slightly. *Note: Read manufacturer's directions and cautions before using dye.*

2 **Pour full-strength** dye into squeeze bottles. Starting with lightest shade at top, squeeze dye onto curtain in a zigzag pattern. Use only as much dye as fabric will absorb. Gently knead to work dye into fabric. Repeat, dyeing middle of curtain with medium shade and bottom with darkest shade. Squeeze out excess dye.

3 **To heat-set,** pleat and fold curtain; place in glass pan. Cover with plastic wrap; microwave on high for 8 minutes. Remove and hang to cool. Rinse in cool water.

> #### 4. MATERIALS
> *100 percent cotton or 50/50 poly/cotton blend white sheer curtain*
> *Liquid dye in 3 shades of 1 color*
> *3 plastic squeeze bottles*
> #### TOOLS
> *Newspaper*
> *Plastic to cover work area (such as large garbage bags)*
> *Disposable rubber gloves*
> *Old glass baking dish*
> *Plastic wrap*

DECOUPAGED PRINTS & BORDERS

These British-inspired print rooms give a whole new meaning to "Prints Charming." Use decoupage medium to adhere book pages, botanical prints, calendar pages, or photocopies of favorite images to your walls for an inexpensive version of a classic look.

INSTRUCTIONS

1 **Use either direct images** or color photocopies of images. If a picture has its own frame, cut around frame. If image is unframed, cut out, leaving very little margin; then copy and cut border patterns from clip-art books to create new frames. (Borders may also be stenciled onto wall using purchased border stencils.)

2 **Tape images (and borders, if desired)** to wall with loops of tape, adjusting placement as needed. Lightly draw around corners of each image. Remove and lightly mark wall to note which image goes in each space. Brush decoupage medium onto wrong side of image and press to wall, matching up corner marks. Smooth image to wall with fingers. Seal with decoupage medium, extending medium just beyond image edges onto surrounding wall. Let dry; apply a second coat.

DESIGNTIP ■ The print-room look suggests a certain formality, so for the most pleasing effect, group prints in a symmetrical arrangement (see the silhouettes on this page or the botanical prints on *page 19, bottom*). If you use prints of varying sizes, like those on *page 19, top*, arrange them in an orderly, evenly spaced pattern and use stenciled borders to organize them into groups. To add dimension, attach real frames over decoupaged images, using purchased frames or making your own from stock molding.

This treatment is more permanent than wallpaper. If you want to remove the prints later to paint or paper the walls, you'll need to use an electric sander.

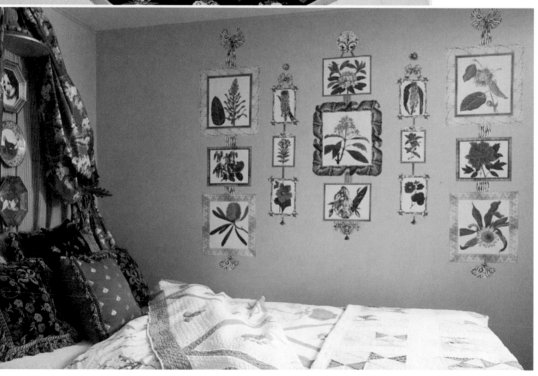

FABRIC WAINSCOT

MATERIALS

*Flat bed sheets (or 2
    coordinating fabrics
    34 inches by 1½ times
    the length you'll be
    covering)*
*1-inch-wide grosgrain
    ribbon the same length
    as fabric*
*Rug tape the same length
    as fabric*
*Grommets, 2 per yard
    of fabric*
*Cup hooks, 1 for every
    foot of length you'll
    be covering*

TOOLS

Grommet tool

Introduce dimension and softness to plain, boring walls and bring a feeling of luxury and warmth to a room with a fabric wainscot. Using bed sheets speeds up the job. If you make the wainscot reversible, you can change it for the seasons; doubling the fabric lets it drape better, too.

INSTRUCTIONS

1 **If using sheets,** let hemmed top edge fall at floor. Cut and piece sheets or fabrics to make 2 panels of the required length. Stitch lengths, right sides together, with ½-inch seams, leaving an opening for turning. Turn, press, and slip-stitch opening closed. Topstitch grosgrain ribbon to edge of top hem on sheet (or 5 inches from bottom edge if using yard goods). Topstitch rug tape to top edge.

2 **Using grommet tool,** place a grommet every 18 inches along top edge. Screw cup hooks into wall 33 inches up from floor and 12 inches apart. Hang fabric from cup hooks.

DESIGNTIP ■ Use this technique at or near ceiling height for a tented effect. Because it doesn't alter the surfaces permanently, it's perfect for hiding damaged or unattractive walls in a rental house or apartment.

STAMPED CHAIR RAIL

MATERIALS
*Molding for top and
    bottom of chair rail*
*Clear polyurethane
    varnish*
Finish nails
Wood filler
*Leaf-shaped rubber
    stamp*
*2 shades of green
    stamping paint*

TOOLS
Sandpaper
Tape measure
Hard lead pencil
Paintbrushes
Handsaw to cut molding
Hammer
Paper plates
*Small paintbrushes
    or foam paintbrushes*

Add architectural interest to
a room with a chair rail and
a stamped design. Simply
nail molding to the wall,
leaving a space to decorate
with rubber stamps.

INSTRUCTIONS

1 **Mark placement of
bottom chair rail** 33 to 36 inches
up from floor. Mark top of chair
rail 8 inches above that line. Draw
a line where top of bottom molding will fall.

2 **Cut molding to fit walls** and seal
with polyurethane. Set aside to dry.

3 **Practice stamping on cardboard**
or paper before stamping walls.

Squeeze darker green paint onto
paper plate. Brush paint onto stamp,
then press on wall so bottom of
stamp is along marked line. Stamp 2
leaves, skip a space for 1 leaf, stamp 1
leaf, skip 1 space. Repeat pattern,
varying angle of stamp each time.
Clean stamp. Fill in skipped spaces
with leaves in lighter green.

4 **Nail molding to wall** over marked
lines. Fill nail holes and sand smooth.
DESIGNTIP ■ See page 16 for
instructions on using the same type of
stamp to make coordinating curtains.

STRIPES & HEARTS PAINTED RUG

Turn a plain white rug into a custom-colored welcome mat with acrylic paints or fabric paints. Look for the paints at crafts and art-supply stores, and check the label to make sure they can be heat-set.

INSTRUCTIONS

1 **Check paint label for use on fabrics.** Some paints must have fabric medium added to make them color-fast on fabric.

2 **Wash rug and let dry.** Draw rug dimensions onto graph paper and draw design to scale. For the 22×34-inch rug shown *above*, the 4 center stripes measure 2×21 inches. Green stripes measure 2¼×21 inches. End stripes measure 2×22 inches. Border blocks measure 4¼×4½ inches.

3 **With pencil and ruler, transfer** design onto rug. Use heart stencil as template to draw hearts in end borders. Referring to photo for guidance and starting at center of rug, paint each section and fringe.

4 **Heat-set and launder** according to paint manufacturer's instructions.

MATERIALS
*Tightly-woven white
    cotton rug*
*Opaque acrylic or fabric
    paints in the following
    colors (or as desired):
    red, yellow, green, orange,
    blue, purple*
*½- and 1-inch flat
    bristle brushes
    (for painting fabric)*
Purchased heart stencil

TOOLS
Graph paper
Pencil, ruler

PAINTED FLOOR QUILT

MATERIALS

*Preprimed artists' canvas,
4 inches longer and
wider than desired
rug size*
*Acrylic paints in the
desired colors*
*Nonyellowing water-based
polyurethane varnish*

TOOLS

*Quilt or quilt book for
pattern*
Graph paper
Pencil
Yardstick or straightedge
Painters' tape
Foam paintbrushes
Crafts knife
Rolling pin

Combine two colonial favorites—quilts and floorcloths—in one colorful project. A simple pattern of squares and rectangles is easy to measure off using a yardstick and pencil. Before you begin painting, draw the design on graph paper and use colored pencils to try different arrangements of your chosen hues.

INSTRUCTIONS

1 **Draw desired finished dimensions** of floorcloth onto graph paper. Select quilt pattern and adapt to fit within these measurements. Transfer design to canvas, allowing a 2-inch margin on each side for a hem. Indicate color placement on pattern as a guide.

2 **Starting at center,** tape around blocks of 1 color. Apply 2 or more coats of paint to blocks; let dry. Remove tape; repeat for blocks of second color. Repeat taping and painting until design areas are filled.

3 **Let paint dry at least 24 hours.** Seal with 2 or more coats of polyurethane. Let dry.

4 **From back side,** lightly score 2 inches in from each edge. Fold back hem along scored line. Cut away excess at corners. Roll hem with rolling pin to press in place.

TECHNIQUE TIP ■ For the best results, choose straight-lined quilt designs with simple shapes. To store a painted floorcloth, open out the hem and roll the cloth around a sturdy cardboard tube, painted side out. If stored in a humid area, lay waxed paper or butcher paper on the canvas before rolling it up so the painted surfaces won't stick to each other.

STENCILED FLOORCLOTH

If you like the look of painted floor-cloths but you're not confident of your painting skills, try stenciling. Hundreds of templates are available in a wide variety of styles. Stencil creams are easy and fun to use and can be applied to fabrics, walls, and furniture. Check crafts stores for coordinated border and motif stencils as well as stencil creams and brushes.

INSTRUCTIONS

1 **Lightly draw a line** 2 inches in from each edge to mark outer edge of rug. Mark horizontal and vertical centers of canvas.

2 **Tape off all areas of square nosegay stencil** except leaves and stems. Spray stencil adhesive on back according to manufacturer's directions. Position stencil so top of design falls 2 inches from horizontal center and design center lines up along vertical center. Erase pencil lines in areas to be stenciled. Paint all leaves and stems with both shades of green, blending colors.

3 **To blend colors,** tap brush onto one color, then scrub brush against paper plate to remove most of paint. Scrub brush onto stencil, coloring only part of opening. Repeat process with a second color, covering unpainted area. Using same brush and a circular motion, blend colors together.

4 **Remove tape.** Tape off all leaf and stem areas and area around bow. Stencil bow with blue. Remove tape around bow, then tape off bow.

5 **Stencil center dot** of each flower yellow. Stencil flowers in the following color combinations or as desired: yellow center with purple edges; lavender center with yellow edges; yellow center with red edges; yellow center with orange edges; light red center with dark red edges (use same red, but vary the amount of paint and pressure). Repeat Steps 2 through 5 to stencil motif on remaining half of floorcloth.

6 **For border,** stencil half the flowers with stencil right side up and half with stencil right side down to create mirror images. Always position stencil so larger flower cluster lies closest to outer corner and smaller flowers point toward center of border.

7 **Tape off flowers.** Spray stencil adhesive on back. Starting with one short end of floorcloth, press stencil to canvas, aligning stencil edge with marked outer edge of rug. Stencil leaves and stems. Repeat taping off

MATERIALS
28×40-inch piece preprimed artists' canvas
Precut square pansy nosegay stencil, about 11×11 inches
Coordinating precut stencil border, about 5×12 inches
Spray stencil adhesive (not spray glue)
Stencil cream in the following colors: garden green, dark hunter green, royal blue, amethyst purple, lavender, sunflower yellow, orange, black cherry
8 small stencil brushes
Brush cleaner or baby oil
Spray sealer or top coat for stencil paint
Nonyellowing polyurethane varnish (optional)

TOOLS
Ruler or yardstick
Hard lead pencil
Artists' kneaded eraser
Painters' tape
Paper plates
Crafts knife, scissors
Rolling pin

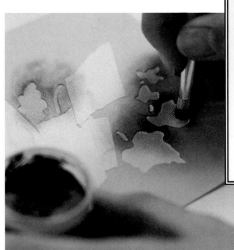

and stenciling to complete flowers. Move stencil to opposite corner and repeat. To stencil long sides, center stencil on one half of border and repeat taping and stenciling. Repeat for opposite side.

8 **Remove tape** from stencil and clean with baby oil or brush cleaner to remove all paint and adhesive residue. Dry stencil completely. Flop design and repeat taping and stenciling to complete corners and long sides.

9 **Let paint dry** for at least 2 days. Erase all pencil lines. Spray canvas with 2 or more coats of top coat spray. If floorcloth will be in a high-traffic area, apply additional coats or let top coat dry for a week and seal with nonyellowing water-based polyurethane varnish.

10 **When top coat** dries, turn floorcloth right side down. Lightly score 2 inches from each edge. Fold canvas back along score lines and roll with rolling pin to form hem. Miter corners by clipping away excess canvas.

■ SISAL RUGS

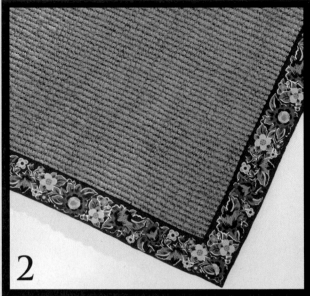

1. DYED SISAL BLOCKS

Brighten a laundry room or enclosed porch with a patchwork of color, achieved with fabric dyes. Repeat each color at least twice for a look that's visually strong.

INSTRUCTIONS

1 **Cut squares apart.** Mix fabric dye with 2 quarts hot water. For stronger colors, use 2 boxes of dye per 2 quarts water. Wearing rubber gloves, immerse square into dye. After 5 to 10 minutes, or when color is slightly darker than desired, remove and let excess dye drain. Lay on newspapers to dry overnight. Repeat with remaining squares, cleaning dye pan with bleach between colors.

2 **Arrange squares** on floor in desired pattern. Sew together with heavy thread or dental floss, using existing holes in sisal as needle holes.

1. MATERIALS
Maize or sisal rug made of 12-inch squares
Powdered fabric dye
Heavy string or dental floss for reattaching squares

TOOLS
Small scissors
Pan for dyeing (cannot be used for food later)
Rubber gloves
Newspapers
Bleach
Heavy large-eye needle

2. FABRIC-BANDED COIR

Border a plain coir rug with fabric used elsewhere in your room, or choose a heavy upholstery fabric that coordinates with your furnishings. A small print works best.

INSTRUCTIONS

1 **The larger the rug,** the wider the band should be. For a 4×6-foot rug, use a 4-inch band. Cut fabric strips twice band width plus 2 inches for hems; cut 2 strips the length of long sides and 2 strips the length of short sides, adding 4 inches to each. Press strips in half lengthwise; this fold will fit against edge of rug.

2 **Press under** 1 inch on each long edge and fold bands over edges of rug. If desired, tack with hot glue. Slip-stitch bands to rug using double strand of thread. At corners, fold excess fabric on diagonal, making a mock miter. Trim away excess and slip-stitch in place.

3 **If rug will be used in high traffic area,** stitch fabric to back of rug in same manner. Otherwise, glue edge in place with commercial-strength glue and let dry completely.

2. MATERIALS
Coir or other solid-woven sisal rug
Fabric for band
Carpet thread to match fabric
Commercial-strength glue (optional)

TOOLS
Hot-glue gun and glue sticks (optional)
Heavy large-eye needle
Thimble

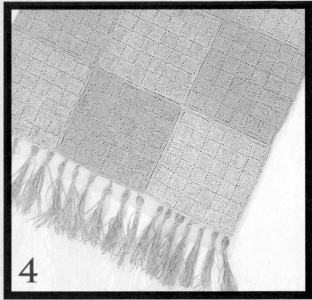

3. STENCILED SISAL

The squares that make up a sisal rug are perfect for stenciling. Copy a design from fabric or buy a precut stencil. Use paint rather than stencil cream for a sharper image.

INSTRUCTIONS

1 **Cut stencil designs,** if desired, from plastic sheet as directed on *page 50.* Cut separate stencil for each color to be used.

2 **Mix paint** with equal amounts of water to dilute. Tape off border strips on rug and paint. Let dry; remove tape.

3 **Tape first stencil in place.** Dab paint through stencil until shape is solidly colored. Because of rug's rough texture, lines and colors won't be perfectly even. Repeat in each square until all of first color has been applied. Repeat for remaining colors. Paint any fine lines freehand.

4 **After paint dries,** protect from chipping by applying nonyellowing floor wax with paint roller.

3. MATERIALS

Precut stencil or
* plastic stencil sheet*
Latex or high-quality
* acrylic paint in desired*
* colors*
Nonyellowing floor wax

TOOLS

Crafts knife
Painters' tape
1-inch foam
* paintbrushes*
Fine paintbrush
* (optional)*
Paint roller and cover

4. CHECKED & FRINGED

A fringe of hand-tied tassels adds a fillip of fun to a dyed checkerboard sisal rug.

INSTRUCTIONS

1 **Cut apart, dye, and reassemble rug** squares as for Dyed Sisal Blocks, *page 26,* forming a checkerboard. If necessary, dye raffia to match.

2 **To make tassels,** loop 1 strand of raffia around cardboard 15 times. Slip a 10-inch length of raffia under loops on 1 edge of cardboard and tie tightly. Slide loops off cardboard.

3 **Cut a 20-inch strand** of raffia and wrap it tightly around raffia loops 1 inch from top to form head of tassel. Knot ends. Cut bottom loops and trim ends even.

4 **Use large needle to thread** and tie tassels to rug, spacing 2 inches apart.

TIP ■ Vacuum sisal with a soft bristle brush or take outdoors and hose with water. Let dry completely.

4. MATERIALS

Maize or sisal rug
* made of 12-inch*
* squares*
Powdered fabric dye
Heavy string or dental
* floss for reattaching*
* squares*
Natural or dyed raffia

TOOLS

Small scissors
Pan for dyeing
* (cannot be used for*
* food later)*
Rubber gloves
Newspapers
Heavy large-eye needle
7-inch length of heavy
* cardboard*

WHEN YOUR GRANDMOTHER GOT TIRED of her upholstery, she just slipcovered the sofa and all the chairs. After all, who could afford to toss out perfectly good furniture and start over? That makeover solution still works, and fortunately it's easier than ever. For one thing, slipcovers don't have to be fitted anymore. Loose-fitting covers that tie in place are easy to sew and suit today's more casual lifestyles. Reupholstering occasional chairs is simpler, too, using a staple gun and hot glue instead of tacks and white glue.

CHAIRS & OTTOMANS

The fabrics you choose for dressing seating pieces help define the new mood. For a breezy, contemporary look, choose white cotton duck. If your drapery and sofa fabrics are florals, update them by covering a chair in a snappy check or stripe. If, on the other hand, your love seat wears an orderly geometric pattern, slipcover an ottoman and pillows in a floral for a softer, more romantic feeling.

Perk up the dining room with flirty little apron slipcovers for the chairs. They're so easy to make, you could stitch a set for every season: crisp white for summer, a rust stripe for fall, a floral for spring, and red-and-green check for a holiday party.

EASY-FIT ARMCHAIR SLIPCOVER

MATERIALS

Paper, muslin, or old sheet
   for pattern
Fabric (to determine
   yardage, see instructions)
Cording to make piping
   (or use purchased piping)
Thread to match fabric

TOOLS

Tape measure
Pencil
Scissors
Zipper foot attachment

Even the most formal chair assumes a relaxed attitude with these easy-fit slipcovers. Furniture with graceful lines and handsome wood benefits most from the slightly baggy covers.

INSTRUCTIONS

1 **Make patterns for slipcovers,** following the directions below, using paper, muslin, or an old sheet. Use patterns to determine yardage requirements; allow extra to cover cording for piping. For cording, allow enough to go around seat, twice around back, and around each arm piece, plus 1 yard.

2 **Unless otherwise stated,** sew all fabric pieces with right sides together using ½-inch seam allowances. Cut and piece 2-inch-wide bias strips and cover cording.

3 **Measure chair seat to widest points** at edge of seat (dotted line on **Diagram 1**). Add 2 inches to each side. Cut paper to these dimensions.

4 **Place paper on seat** and trace around outside edge and around arm and leg posts. Cut pattern 1 inch larger all around (see **Diagram 2**) Using pattern, cut seat from fabric.

5 **Sew piping around seat** along seam line. Clip corners at leg and arm notches almost to seam line. Turn raw edges of

notches under and topstitch close to cording, using zipper foot.

6 **For skirt,** cut 4 pieces the depth of chair seat front plus 3 inches (see **Diagram 1**). For length, refer to **Diagram 2** and measure from points A to B (front), B to D (side), C to D (back), and A to C (side). Add 2 inches to each length.

7 **For each skirt piece,** hem 1 long and both short sides. Mark center of remaining long edge and center of each seat section. Pin skirt pieces to matching seat sections, matching ends, centers, and raw edges. Stitch along seam line, close to piping.

8 **Cut 8 ties,** each 2×19 inches. Fold in short ends. Fold long edges to meet in center, wrong sides together. Fold in half again, encasing all raw edges. Tie should now measure ½×18 inches. Topstitch all around. Sew ties to seat at piping line, placing at opposing sides of each opening.

9 **For arm covers,** measure arm piece (see **Diagram 3**) and add 2 inches to all sides. Make pattern, rounding corners slightly. If chair does not have padded arm section and you want one, wrap part of arm tightly with several layers of quilt batting and tack in place with heavy-duty thread. Cover tightly with muslin and slip-stitch in place.

10 **Cut fabric arm covers.** Fit fabric over arm, wrong side up. Pin darts

at each corner for better fit. Stitch darts. Turn to right side. Sew piping around arm pieces, matching raw edges. Turn under raw edges and topstitch close to piping.

11 **Make eight 2x13-inch ties** as for seat. Sew to arm cover corners.

12 **For chair back,** measure front (see **Diagram 1**) and add 1 inch to all sides. Repeat for back. Cut papers to these dimensions. Fit and trace on chair back as for seat. Cut pattern 1 inch larger than marked lines. Referring to **Diagram 1**, mark point A (top of arm), point B (center top), and point C (top of other arm).

13 **Cut out fabric.** Sew piping around each piece, matching raw edges and seam lines.

14 **For side panel,** measure depth of back at widest point; add 1 inch. For length, measure across top of chair from point A to point C (see **Diagram 1**); add 2 inches. Hem short ends. Sew 1 long edge to back piece, matching points A, C, and centers. Sew front to side panel. If front is smaller than back, make small darts in panel for smooth fit.

15 **Turn under raw edges** of front and back from A, around bottom, to C. Topstitch along piping.

16 **Cut and sew 4 ties** as for seat. Sew to front and back pieces directly under chair arm.

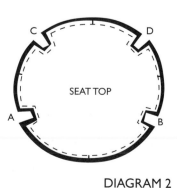

DIAGRAM 1

DIAGRAM 2

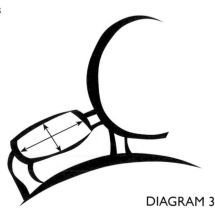

DIAGRAM 3

APRON SLIPCOVER FOR DINING CHAIR

MATERIALS

*Paper or muslin
    for pattern*
Fabric
*Thread to match
    fabric*

TOOLS

Tape measure
Pencil
Scissors

INSTRUCTIONS

1 **Measure chair seat** side to side at widest point; add 4 inches (see **Diagram 1**). Measure front to back at widest point; add 3 inches. Cut pattern from paper.

2 **Fit pattern to chair seat.** Clip and trace around legs (see **Diagram 2**), then cut along dotted lines. Add ½-inch seam allowances to leg areas. Using pattern, cut apron from fabric. Hem all straight edges.

3 **Cut 2 bias strips,** each 2×40 inches. Fold under ½ inch on all sides. Fold strip in half lengthwise, wrong sides together. Topstitch from each end, leaving 10 inches open in center. Slip open section of strip over raw edge of leg opening, encasing the raw edge. Topstitch in place. Tie seat cover over seat.

LEFT AND BELOW: *The apron tucks over the seat at the back to meet the wooden frame. Ties keep the slipcover in place.*

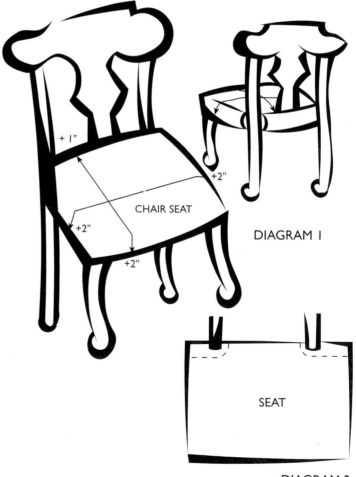

+1"

+2"

+2"

CHAIR SEAT

+2"

DIAGRAM 1

SEAT

DIAGRAM 2

FITTED SLIPCOVER FOR A CHAIR

Turn a plain upholstered occasional chair into cottage-style seating with a floral skirt and plaid topper. Cover a pair of dining chairs in this style for a dressy look in the dining room, and bring them into the living room whenever you need extra seating.

INSTRUCTIONS

1 **Fabric yardage varies with** size and style of chair. Measure each chair, then buy extra to allow for matching. As a guideline, the chair shown here (44 inches tall with 20×22-inch seat) took 2½ yards 54-inch-wide chintz for gathered skirt, 3 yards 54-inch-wide plaid for chair back and seat, ½ yard drapery lining, and 6⅛ yards cording.

2 **Use T pins to secure fabric** to chair for measuring and cutting. Use dressmakers' pins for all sewing. Baste all seams first, check fit, then stitch. Fit should be perfect, so expect to rip out seams and refit pieces. Unless otherwise stated, seam allowances are 1 inch.

3 **To make piping,** piece 2½-inch-wide bias strips of fabric and cover cording, leaving 1-inch flange.

4 **Drape chair-cover fabric, right side out,** over front of chair back, making sure pattern is centered and straight (see **Photo 1,** *page 36*). Pin with T pins. Cut away excess fabric, leaving 4-inch margin.

5 **Pin piping to fabric on chair along edge** of chair with piping toward center of fabric and flange toward margin. Pin piping to fabric every 4 inches, taking care not to catch original upholstery (see **Photo 2,** *page 37*).

6 **Remove fabric from chair.** Stitch piping to fabric using zipper foot, stitching close to cording. Trim away margin, leaving 1-inch seam allowance.

MATERIALS
Coordinating fabrics for
  skirt and chair cover
Cording
Thread to match fabrics
Heavy-duty thread
3 yards of twill tape or
  grosgrain ribbon
Hook-and-loop fasteners

TOOLS
T pins
Dressmakers' pins
Scissors
Tape measure
Sewing needle
Compass
Zipper foot attachment
Pinking shears

7 **Repeat steps 4 through 6 to make outside of chair back.** Turn both pieces wrong side out and fit to chair. Pin in place. To join front and outside back pieces, cut side panel; width should equal depth of chair back plus 2 inches for seam allowances. For length, measure sides and top of chair back. Pin panel to front piece, then to outside back with right sides facing (see **Photo 3**). Stitch. Trim seam allowances.

8 **To hem chair-back cover,** open out piping casing at bottom corners. Snip off cording to finished hemline. Turn bottom edge of cover under twice and topstitch.

9 **For bows,** cut 2 strips 5×48 inches. Turn under ½ inch on all edges. Press in half lengthwise, wrong sides facing, and topstitch all around. Machine-tack midpoint of each bow to front side seam 1 to 2 inches from hemmed edge.

10 **Slide slipcover over chair back** (see **Photo 4**). Tie bows.

11 **For scalloped apron,** cut fabric strip 6 inches wide by perimeter of chair seat plus 3 inches for overlap. Use compass to draw half-circles on bottom edge; cut out. Repeat for drapery lining. Sew lining to fabric along scalloped edge, right sides facing. Clip curves, turn, and press. Turn under ½ inch on ends; press and topstitch. Baste raw edges together.

12 **To determine width of skirt,** measure perimeter of chair seat and add 3 inches, then double this figure. For depth, measure from 2 inches below top of seat to floor; add 2½ inches for seam allowance and hem. Cut and piece fabric to make panel of these dimensions. Hem short edges with narrow hems. For bottom hem, turn under ½ inch, then 1 inch; top-

stitch. Using heavy-duty thread, gather top edge (see **Photo 5**). Adjust gathers to fit raw edge of scalloped piece. Stitch twill tape or ribbon under gathering stitches to stabilize gathers. Baste piping to top of scalloped strip, raw edges matching. Sew scalloped strip to top of skirt along seam line, raw edges matching (see **Photo 6**).

13 **For seat cover,** pin and fit fabric over seat, wrong side up. Measure seat from back to tops of front legs, then side to side. Pin and sew darts at front corners. Clip and cut out around back posts. Line raw edges of post cutouts with bias strips of fabric. Hem bottom and back edges.

14 **To attach skirt,** fit seat cover to chair, right side out. Fold seam allowance of skirt under. Starting at back corner, pin skirt to chair along sides and front. Lift skirt and pin seam allowances to seat cover with dressmaker pins. Remove T pins and seat cover; stitch skirt panel to seat. Do not pin or sew skirt panel to seat cover in back.

15 **Cut hook-and-loop tape** same width as seat back. Handsew 1 strip to outside lower back edge of seat. Sew remaining strip to skirted panel.

16 **To attach seat slipcover,** fit cutouts around back posts. Pull overlap on skirted panel around back corner, tuck flange down, and pin to old upholstery (see **Photo 7**). Wrap skirted panel across back, tuck seam allowance down, and secure panel top to bottom back of seat cover with hook-and-loop strips. Pin panel end over back corner overlap. Lift skirt and pin seam allowance to seat to prevent slipping.

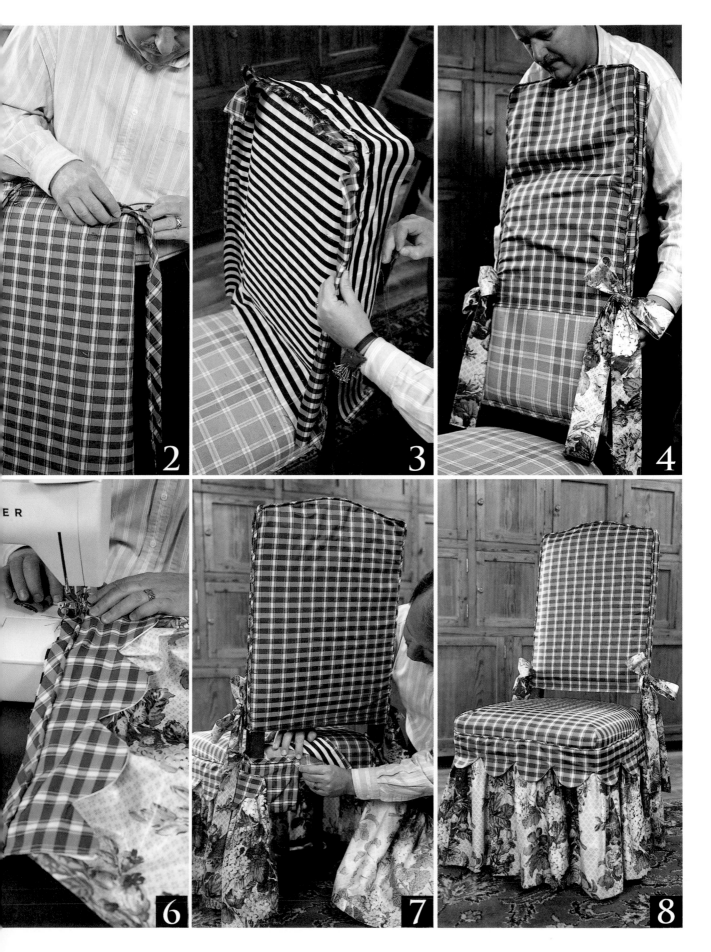

BLANKET-COVERED SIDE CHAIR

Transform flea market finds like
this chair with fabric. Tapestry
would be pretty but predictable—
jazz up your room with an
unexpected fabric choice.

Cozy up a nondescript chair
with a warm, fleecy covering.
Use blanket fabric or polar
fleece yardage, or cut up a
purchased blanket. Be sure to
make the most of the fabric's
pattern by centering it on
both seat and back.

INSTRUCTIONS

1 **Remove old upholstery**
and use it to make patterns
for seat and chair back, or
cut patterns from paper.

2 **For chair back,** center
fabric on front and pin to
hold in position. Working
alternately from top to bottom and side to side, pull
fabric to back and staple to
chair frame. Cut a piece to
fit back, covering stapled edges. Turn
under raw edges and glue in place.

3 **For seat,** clip and turn under fabric
around leg posts. Pull edges of seat cover
to bottom of seat, taking care not to dis-
tort pattern. Staple to underside of seat.
Trim excess fabric.

TACK-TRIMMED
PARSONS CHAIR

MATERIALS

*Upholstered chair with
    wooden frame for tacking*
*Tacks, about $^7/_{16}$ inch in
    diameter (about 200 for
    chair shown)*
*2 larger (about $^5/_8$ inch) tacks
    for accents*

TOOLS

Tissue paper
Dressmakers' pins
Pencil
Hammer

Sometimes it's good to be tacky. The pure, simple lines of this upholstered chair are perfect for embellishing with a wavy row of tacks. Other furniture works well for tack trim, too, provided there's a wooden surface to nail into.

INSTRUCTIONS

1 **Enlarge and extend** pattern below to fit chair. Trace onto tissue paper and pin to sides of chair.

2 **Hammer tacks loosely through paper.** Tear away paper and hammer tacks all the way in.

As an accent, use a $^5/_8$-inch tack on each side of the chair where the back meets the seat.

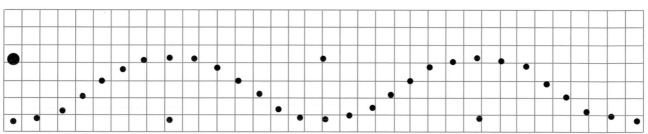

I SQUARE = $^1/_2$"

Rug-Covered Footstools

Check flea markets and secondhand stores for footstools, or buy an unfinished three-legged stool at a hardware store. Cover it with old rug scraps for a new footrest.

INSTRUCTIONS

1 **Pad top of stool with several layers of quilt batting.** For thicker padding, cut upholstery foam slightly larger than stool top. Tack to top with hot glue. Stretch batting over padded top and staple to edge.

2 **Cut rug fabric larger than top.** Note: Never cut up good-quality antique rugs. Look for inexpensive new or reproduction pieces or use the good spots of an otherwise worn-out rug. Stretch the rug over the padded top and staple to the base edge, pleating or tucking the fabric to fit.

3 **For stool with pleated fabric skirt,** cut skirt band the length of stool legs plus hem and double the circumference. Hem 1 long edge. Evenly space and press pleats. Glue long raw edge over edge of rug top. Trim excess fabric at end; turn under raw edge and tack in place.

4 **Glue fringe or trim over** raw edge of rug or skirt fabric.

MATERIALS
Small footstool for covering
Rug scraps
Upholstery foam (optional)
Quilt batting
Fringe or fabric trim

TOOLS
Scissors
Staple gun and staples
Hot-glue gun and
   glue sticks

FRINGED CHINTZ TUFFET

MATERIALS
12-inch plywood circle
Three 6-inch-long
  purchased furniture legs
14-inch round pillow form
Quilt batting
¾ yard of fabric
Large washer
4-inch-long screw to fit
  washer
1¼ yard of 6-inch-long
  fringe
1¼ yard of 3-inch-long
  fringe
Button to cover

TOOLS
Drill
Hot-glue gun and
  glue sticks
Staple gun and staples
Scissors

Make this tuffet for your Miss Muffet from three lumberyard legs, a plywood round, and a purchased pillow form. Who would guess such utilitarian makings could give a room such a whimsical, feminine touch?

INSTRUCTIONS

1 **Attach legs to plywood,** spacing evenly around circumference. Center pillow over plywood; tack in place with hot glue. Stretch batting over pillow. Staple to edges of plywood as shown *at right.* Staple fabric over batting. Trim away excess fabric and batting.

2 **Center washer over stool.** Screw through washer and into plywood, creating dimple for button. Cover button with scrap of fabric. Glue over washer.

3 **Use hot glue to attach 6-inch fringe to edge** of plywood, covering raw edge of fabric. Glue 3-inch fringe over 6-inch fringe.

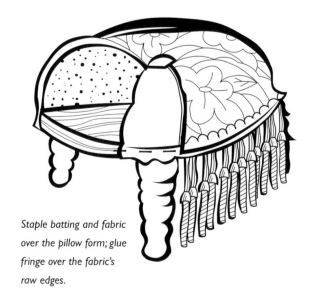

Staple batting and fabric over the pillow form; glue fringe over the fabric's raw edges.

SLIPCOVERED OTTOMAN

MATERIALS
Square or rectangular ottoman
Cording
Upholstery fabric
Thread and heavy-duty thread to match fabric
Twill tape or ribbon
Hook-and-loop tape

TOOLS
Tape measure
Scissors
T pins and dressmakers' pins
Sewing needle

Bring a more romantic feeling to a trim and tailored setting by covering an old ottoman with a gathered-skirt slipcover. Or, look for a new ottoman on sale at a furniture store and cover it to match your room.

INSTRUCTIONS

1 **Fabric yardage will vary** with size and style of ottoman. Measure piece as directed below; allow extra fabric for matching pattern, if necessary. Unless otherwise stated, sew with right sides together and use ½-inch seam allowances. Slipcover is made in 3 pieces: top, band, and skirt.

2 **To make piping,** piece 2½-inch-wide bias strips of fabric to equal twice the perimeter of ottoman plus 8 inches. Cover cording, leaving ½ inch flange beyond cording.

3 **Cut top from fabric,** adding seam allowance to each side. For band width, measure cushion depth plus 1 inch for seams. For length, measure perimeter; add 6 inches for overlap. Cut and piece fabric for band.

4 **For skirt, measure from bottom** of cushion to floor. Add 3 inches (2½ inches for hem and ½-inch seam allowance). Double ottoman perimeter for length. Cut and piece skirt.

5 **Cut piping in half.** Sew one half to top along stitching line. Sew remaining piping to bottom edge of band.

6 **Hem lower edge of skirt.** Gather upper edge with heavy-duty thread. Pull up gathers so skirt fits band. Sew twill tape or ribbon under gathering thread to stabilize gathers. Sew gathered edge of skirt to piped edge of band, keeping raw edges even.

7 **On each opening,** turn under 1 inch; turn under 1 inch again and topstitch in place. Fit band to ottoman top, overlapping opening about 1 inch. Position opening in middle of 1 side. Sew hook-and-loop fasteners to opening edges.

WHEN DRESSED IN FRESH COLOR OR pattern, tables, chests, and armoires can redefine the character of a space. They're functional pieces you're likely to be using every day. So why not have some fun with the decorative treatment you apply to them?

Painting and stenciling are the easiest ways to transform unfinished and secondhand furniture, and wallpaper offers some wonderful options, too. Use borders or cut motifs from wallpaper to create a handpainted look or to coordinate the piece with papered walls.

FURNITURE
IDEAS

Unless you're creating a complete, matching set of furniture—like the cottage-style suites that were popular in the late 19th century—you probably won't want to have more than one or two such specialty pieces in a room. Cast them in a starring role against a background of warm wood or clean white to make a clear statement of personal style.

To learn how to dress up a vanity or tabletop with pressed leaves— or with a collection of special mementos—see page 59. This is a good way to hide a marred surface or simply to give a temporary facelift to an old piece of furniture.

HARLEQUIN DINING TABLE

A classic diamond pattern turns a ho-hum tabletop into a lively surface for dining, playing cards, or writing grocery lists. Use a sea sponge to pat the paint onto the border and every other row of diamonds for distinctive texture. Apply several coats of polyurethane to the finished piece for everyday durability.

INSTRUCTIONS

1 **Wipe table clean.** If using an unfinished table, first seal with clear acrylic sealer.

2 **Draw table dimensions** onto graph paper. Draw an inner rectangle that is divisible by 5 on the short sides and by 6 on the long sides, centering it in the first rectangle. The space between the 2 rectangles will be the sponged and painted borders.

3 **On inner rectangle,** divide short sides into 5 equal sections and long sides into 6 equal sections. Also mark the midpoint of each section.

4 **Starting at one corner,** connect midpoints with diagonal lines to form diamonds. If diamonds are distorted, add or subtract rows of diamonds or adjust border. When satisfied with design, lightly transfer it to tabletop with a hard lead pencil and straightedge. Mark a ½-inch border around diamond design.

5 **Mask off outermost border** by applying painters' tape along line. Seal tape to table with a rigid plastic card. To sponge paint, tear a natural sea sponge into small pieces, about 2×3 inches. Dip sponge into 1 color of paint, then blot onto a paper plate to remove excess.

When sponge is almost dry, dab it onto tabletop in an uneven pattern. Reload sponge as it dries and continue sponging. Repeat with remaining 2 colors.

6 **After border dries,** remove tape and mask off both

sides of ½-inch border. Paint it in one solid color and let dry. Referring to diagram *below,* tape off rows of diamonds and paint in solid colors, alternating colors randomly. Tape each diamond separately to keep edges clean and sharp. Apply two coats of paint, if necessary. Repeat until all solid diamonds have been painted.

7 **Tape and sponge-paint** remaining diamonds, alternating colors randomly and using only one color in each diamond. Do not paint partial diamonds along edges.

8 **Let paint dry.** Seal table with two or more coats of polyurethane.

9 **To clean table,** wipe with a damp cloth, then dry with a towel.

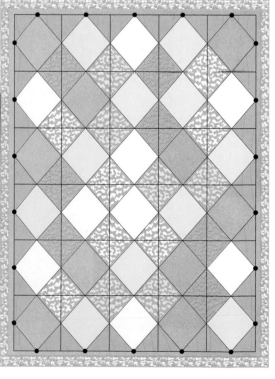

ABOVE AND RIGHT: *Coordinate the harlequin design with your room by choosing one or two colors from upholstery or curtain fabric, then add a tint or tone of one of them. Or, start with your wall color and add two related hues. Follow the diagram at right for painting the design.*

PAINTED PLAID SIDEBOARD

Painting a plaid design is easier than you think: simply draw off vertical and horizontal rows of varying widths, and paint the resulting rectangles with closely related colors of paint.

INSTRUCTIONS

1 **Remove all doors, drawers, and hardware.** Prime and paint body and legs of piece (but not top) in 2 desired colors.

2 **Using diagram *below* as a guide,** draw horizontal and vertical lines to make rows of varying widths on doors, drawer fronts, and top. Leave an unpainted border on each.

3 **Label 4 shades of paint 1, 2, 5, and 6.** Number 3 is metallic gold and 4 is wood stain. Working vertically, lightly number each square on doors, drawer fronts, and top with pencil as shown in diagram *below*.

4 **Run painters' tape around** all number 1 blocks. Apply matte medium to tape's inner edge to keep paint from seeping under tape; apply medium to block. Let dry; paint blocks with number 1 paint. After paint dries, remove tape.

5 **Repeat for colors 2, 3, 5, and 6.**

6 **Tape around number 4 blocks and borders.** Rub walnut stain onto raw wood. Seal plaid-painted areas with 2 coats of polyurethane varnish, sanding lightly between coats.

TECHNIQUETIP ■ If you're not sure of your color combination, test the pattern on paper first to make sure it produces the desired plaid effect.

1	3	5	1	3	5
2	4	6	2	4	6
1	3	5	1	3	5
2	4	6	2	4	6
1	3	5	1	3	5
2	4	6	2	4	6

STENCILED SIDEBOARD

MATERIALS

Painted or unfinished
  sideboard or similar
  furniture
Paint for base coat
Stencil plastic
8×10 inch piece of glass
Spray stencil adhesive
  (not spray glue)
Hunter green artist-
  quality acrylic paint
  in tube
Stencil brushes
Nonyellowing water-
  based sealer

TOOLS

Sandpaper
Tack cloth
Artists' tape
Soft lead pencil
Ruler or yardstick
Crafts knife
Small paintbrush
Paper plates
Baby oil or brush
  cleaner for cleaning
  stencil

You can never have too much storage. A sideboard in the dining room holds table linens and serving pieces. In the living room, it stashes books and magazines and can display collectibles, providing a focal point for the room. Or, in an entry, a sideboard offers a handy place to drop mail and hide clutter.

INSTRUCTIONS

1 **Prime and paint sideboard,** sanding lightly between coats. Wipe with tack cloth. Using soft lead pencil, lightly draw stencil placement lines around top, 1½ inches from edge.

2 **Using a photocopier, enlarge** bamboo border and bamboo grass patterns on *page 51* to fit furniture. For sideboard shown *above*, border was enlarged by 220 percent and grasses by 165 percent. To change length of border sections, adjust straight segments between crossed ends to desired length.

3 **Place border pattern under glass.** Tape stencil plastic over glass. Cut out stencil design with crafts knife. Repeat for grass pattern. Spray backs of stencils with stencil adhesive according to manufacturer's directions.

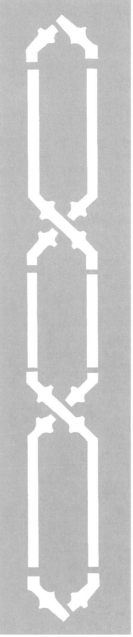

4 **Place center of border stencil** at center of sideboard top with border's lower edge along placement line. Squeeze a small amount of paint onto paper plate. Dip brush into paint, then tap onto plate to remove most of paint. When brush is almost dry, tap brush over stencil openings in a pouncing motion, keeping brush vertical. Reload brush as needed. Design will be more interesting if color is slightly uneven.

5 **Peel away stencil** and repeat process across front of sideboard. Plan ahead so corner of stencil falls at corner of sideboard, elongating design as needed. Turn corner and position stencil so corners are at right angles. Stencil along side, then back and remaining side. After paint dries, remove pencil lines with soap and water or art eraser.

6 **For drawers, center and stencil border design** on drawer panels.

7 **For doors, center grass design** on door and stencil as for borders. Wash paint off stencil with soap, then remove adhesive residue with baby oil or brush cleaner. Dry completely. Spray stencil adhesive on right side of stencil to reverse it; center and apply stencil to other door.

8 **Paint knobs** with strokes and dots, if desired.

9 **Let paint dry at least 24 hours.** Apply 2 coats of sealer to all surfaces.

TECHNIQUETIP ■ Use a cotton swab dipped in rubbing alcohol to repair slips, leaks, and other unwanted stencil paint lines. Then wipe the area clean with a moist paper towel or baby wipe.

CRACKLE-FINISH WINDSOR BENCH

At one time, the only way to create the aged finish of crackled paint was to use hide glue, a messy and unpredictable procedure. Now it's easy to get authentic-looking results using crackle medium—a clear, thick liquid available at crafts stores and home improvement centers.

MATERIALS
Unfinished or secondhand bench
Primer
Acrylic paint: black and white
Crackle medium (available at crafts stores)
Clear water-based varnish

TOOLS
Sandpaper
Tack cloth
Paintbrushes

INSTRUCTIONS

1 Sand entire bench well. Wipe with tack cloth, then apply primer. Let dry and sand again.

2 Paint entire bench black. Let dry; apply a second coat if necessary.

3 After black paint has dried, apply crackle medium to seat of bench, following manufacturer's instructions. Let dry until it's tacky to touch: when you can leave a fingerprint in medium, it's dry enough.

4 Starting at one end and following grain of wood, quickly brush white paint over seat. Do not rebrush an area after applying paint. As paint dries, cracks will appear. Let paint dry completely; seal with varnish.

TECHNIQUE TIP ■ Although most crackle mediums work the same way, the finished effect varies with the brand you buy. Read and follow the manufacturer's instructions; for best results use the same manufacturer's paints. For fine cracks, apply a thin coat of crackle medium; for larger cracks, apply a thicker coat. The direction in which you brush on the top coat of paint determines the direction of the cracks. For long cracks that follow the grain of the wood, make long, straight strokes; it takes practice to achieve an authentic look. Creating a web of cracks is easier: Apply the top coat of paint with short, slip-slap brush strokes, varying the direction in which you brush with each stroke.

The direction of your brush stroke determines the direction of crackling. Cracks appear as the top coat of paint dries.

PAINTED LACE TABLE RUNNER

Use inexpensive lace fabric and spray paint to give instant personality to a small table. Unlike real lace, this table runner won't slip or slide and washes with the wipe of a cloth.

INSTRUCTIONS

The lace table runner in this project will be covered with paint and spray stencil adhesive. Choose a piece that has little monetary and no emotional value.

1 **Spray wrong side of lace** with spray stencil adhesive according to manufacturer's directions. Press it into place on table. To wrap fabric over edge of table as shown *at right*, drape fabric over edge of table and cut it even with bottom edge of tabletop. Press remainder of lace onto apron of table. Do not wrap lace around lip of table; this will cause too much distortion in the design.

2 **Using painters' tape,** create a ¼- to ½-inch-wide border of exposed wood around outer edge of table runner, positioning tape so it is parallel to outer edge of lace. Cover rest of table with kraft paper to protect it from drifting spray paint.

3 **Spray white spray paint evenly** over lace. Let paint dry, then remove lace, tape, and paper. After paint dries completely, seal with 2 coats of clear acrylic spray sealer.

TECHNIQUETIP ■ Spray stencil adhesives (not spray glue) work on many fabric and paper doilies, eliminating the need for tape. Following the manufacturer's directions, spray the wrong side of the lace, then press it to a test surface. Gently peel it away to make sure it can be removed completely. If so, apply it to your work surface. There's no need to reapply the stencil adhesive.

> **MATERIALS**
> *Heavy lace table runner*
> *Spray stencil adhesive*
>   *(not spray glue)*
> *Kraft or butcher paper*
> *Fast-drying white*
>   *enamel spray paint*
> *Clear acrylic spray sealer*
> **TOOLS**
> *Painters' tape*

DOILY AND LATTICE DRESSER

A paper doily, auto detailing tape, and spray paint are the secret ingredients for giving a plain pine dresser a lacy facelift. Use the same technique to decorate the top or sides of other furniture for the bedroom or bath.

INSTRUCTIONS

1 **Remove drawers and knobs.** Lightly sand and wipe drawers and chest. Using painters' tape, tape off outer ¾ inch of each drawer, wrapping tape around edge of drawer.

2 **Following manufacturer's directions,** use spray stencil adhesive to adhere double layer of doilies to center of each drawer. With auto detailing tape, start in one corner of drawer and run strips of tape diagonally across corner, spacing strips ¼ inch apart (see photo *center left*).

3 **When that corner is complete,** move to next corner and run strips diagonally across corner. The strips bordering lace should meet at a point on center with doily (see photo *center left*). Repeat for opposite side of drawer. Fill in corners with additional strips of tape, forming lattice pattern. Lightly run plastic card over tape to seal it to drawer.

4 **Apply 2 light coats** of spray paint to taped drawers, letting paint dry 1 hour between coats (see photo *bottom left*). After final coat dries 1 hour, carefully remove tape and doilies. Let paint dry completely. Apply 2 coats of clear acrylic sealer to drawers and chest. Reattach knobs.

MATERIALS

*Unfinished pine chest
  of drawers*
*Oval paper doilies to
  fit drawer fronts*
*Spray stencil adhesive
  (not spray glue)*
*¼-inch-wide auto
  detailing tape (available
  at auto body stores)*
*White satin-finish
  spray paint*
Clear acrylic spray sealer

TOOLS

Fine sandpaper
Tack cloth
Painters' tape
Screwdriver
*Rigid plastic strip (such as
  an old credit card)*

STRIPED BLANKET CHEST

MATERIALS

Fabric a few inches
    larger than chest top
3 colors of latex or
    acrylic paint to
    coordinate with fabric
Primer
Light walnut stain
Clear nonyellowing
    water-based
    polyurethane

TOOLS

Screwdriver
Fine sandpaper
Tack cloth
Painters' tape
Staple gun and staples
Paintbrushes
Rigid plastic strip
    (such as an old
    credit card)
Soft lint-free rags

Customize an unfinished padded-top blanket chest with a simple striped design. Leave the beveled edges around the panels and the edge of the seat unpainted to emphasize the stripes.

INSTRUCTIONS

1 **Remove top and hardware.** Wrap fabric around padded top and staple to back side with staple gun.

2 **Mask off all areas** that will not be painted. Prime remaining areas. Sand lightly and wipe clean with tack cloth. Paint main panels and bottom edge with a medium-range hue. Paint remaining sections with lightest hue.

3 **Mask off stripes** on main panels and paint them with the darkest color. Apply a second coat if needed.

4 **Remove tape.** Lightly rub exposed wood with stain. Seal all surfaces with polyurethane, sanding lightly between coats. Replace top and hardware.

DESIGNTIP ■ When choosing paint, don't try to match the fabric exactly. Instead, let the fabric inspire you, and select complementary or coordinating hues. Using color to unify the painted stripes with the fabric top allows you to opt for floral or geometric prints if you prefer them to stripes.

STACKED PAINTED DRESSER

Create your own modern version of a traditional chest-on-chest by stacking two similar chests and painting them to match. You'll increase your storage without taking up any extra floor space.

INSTRUCTIONS

1 **Stacked chests will be more secure** if the top chest is slightly smaller than the bottom chest. If the top one wobbles, bolt it to the bottom one after painting it.

2 **Remove legs from smaller chest.** Remove drawers and hardware from both chests. Sand pieces, then wipe clean with a tack cloth. Paint both chests and all drawers with 2 or more coats of white paint, sanding lightly between coats.

3 **After paint dries,** replace knobs and slip drawers into chests. Stack smaller chest on top of larger chest.

DESIGNTIP ■ White furniture against a white wall expands the room's feeling of light and space. To draw more attention to the piece, paint both chests in colors that contrast with the walls.

MATERIALS
2 similar chests
White paint
Matching knobs
TOOLS
Fine sandpaper
Tack cloth
Paintbrush

LEAF-TOPPED VANITY TABLE

Here's a tabletop you can change on a whim. Arrange leaves, flowers, or even photos and postcards randomly on the table's surface, then weight them under glass. First press leaves or flowers by flattening them between sheets of smooth, absorbent paper. Place them under a stack of books for one to two weeks.

INSTRUCTIONS

1 **Spray hydrangea blossoms** lightly with gold paint and let dry. Lay paper over vanity top. Arrange leaves on paper. Break petals from blossoms and scatter petals over leaves and paper. Lay glass over arrangement.

DESIGNTIP ■ Instead of leaves, try pressed ferns for a botanical-print effect, or change the table for summer with dried flower petals. For a feminine flourish, frame the flower petals with bands of sheer ribbon. Run the ribbons along the vanity edges, securing them with tiny dots of double-stick tape or white glue.

MATERIALS
Parchment, rice, or art paper cut to fit the tabletop
Pressed leaves
Dried hydrangea blossoms
Gold spray paint
½-inch-thick glass with smoothed edges to fit the tabletop

■ARMOIRES

Begin with an unfinished armoire, then customize to your heart's content. Fitted with shelves, drawers, a hanging rod, or a computer tray, an armoire is the ideal storage unit for any room. Use paint, wallpaper, or stencils to decorate the piece in a style that appeals to you and suits the room where you'll use it.

1

1. VINTAGE STYLE
INSTRUCTIONS

1 **Paint entire armoire** white. When paint dries, apply a coat of light blue. Let dry.

2 **Lightly sand** to remove some of top coat, letting base coat show through. Sand areas of normal wear, such as along edges and around knobs, a little more. Wipe cupboard with a tack cloth to remove sanding dust.

3 **Paint a white band** along beveled edge around door panels. Sand it to reveal the blue paint.

4 **Using a purchased alphabet stencil,** trace words for drawer labels onto paper. Use as a pattern to cut words from stencil plastic; center and stencil words on drawers, using acrylic or stencil paint. Draw and cut corner motif in same manner, adjusting a purchased stencil pattern to fit corners of armoire doors. Or paint words and motifs freehand, using a narrow paint brush.

5 **Cut eyelet to fit** shelves and glue in place with a hot-glue gun. To remove eyelet for washing, peel away the glue.

2. NEOCLASSICAL STYLE
INSTRUCTIONS

1 **Paint entire cabinet** light taupe except for outer trim of doors. Paint outer trim of doors dark taupe.

2 **Using a straightedge,** bisect each door panel, creating four triangles on each panel. Mask off upper and lower triangles; leave them light taupe. Seal tape with rigid plastic card. Paint remaining triangles ivory. Let paint dry.

---

1. MATERIALS
Flat latex paint: white, light blue
Acrylic or stencil paint: ivory, dark blue
Purchased stencils
Stencil plastic
Eyelet to fit shelves
TOOLS
Paintbrushes
Fine sandpaper
Tack cloth
Crafts knife
Clean lint-free cloths
Hot-glue gun and glue sticks

---

3 **Divide drawer fronts** into seven equal sections. Use painters' tape to mask off alternating sections and paint ivory, creating wide stripes of ivory and taupe.

4 **Center stencil design** over intersection of door diamonds. Apply stencil adhesive according to manufacturer's directions and press stencil in place. Stencil wreath onto doors with gold stencil cream. Use a dry brush and very little paint to achieve a translucent look.

3. WHIMSICAL STYLE
INSTRUCTIONS

1 **Paint body of armoire** yellow and doors white. Using a straightedge and pencil,

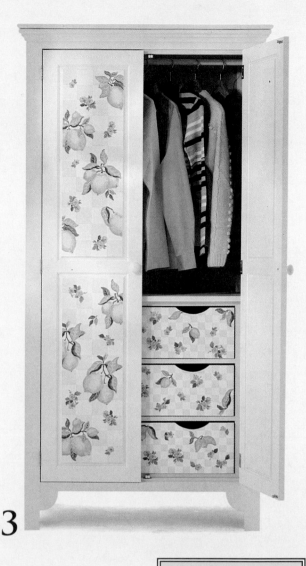

2

3

2. MATERIALS

*Latex paint: dark and
    light taupe, ivory*
*Purchased wreath
    stencil*
Spray stencil adhesive
*Round stiff-bristled
    stencil brush*
Gold stencil cream

TOOLS

Paintbrushes
Hard lead pencil
Yardstick or straightedge
Painters' tape
Rigid plastic card

divide door panels into an even number of squares measuring about 2×2 inches. Divide drawer fronts into 1×1-
inch squares.

2 **Mask off every other square** with painter's tape. Seal
tape to surface with a rigid plastic card. Paint squares yellow, forming a checkerboard design.

3 **Cut out wallpaper motifs,** using larger designs on doors
and smaller ones on drawers. Glue designs to armoire with
white glue. Smooth wallpaper with your fingers or rigid
plastic card. Wipe away excess glue.

4 **When glue dries,** apply two or more coats of
polyurethane to all wallpapered surfaces.

DESIGNTIP ■ When you're cutting paper or plastic
with a crafts knife, tape the paper to a piece of glass and
cut directly on the glass. The knife blade won't slip as
much, and you'll protect your work surface.

3. MATERIALS

*Latex paint: yellow,
    white*
Wallpaper
White glue
*Clear nonyellowing
    water-based
    polyurethane*

TOOLS

Paintbrushes
Hard lead pencil
Yardstick or straightedge
Painters' tape
Rigid plastic strip
Crafts knife
Soft lint-free cloths

TURN AN ORDINARY BED INTO AN inviting retreat with a canopy or curtains. Once required for warmth, these bed dressings now evoke a mood of luxurious privacy. Curtains falling from ceiling to floor add drama and a feeling of enclosure, while a canopy suspended from the ceiling creates a thronelike effect. Installing them over your existing bed is easier than you might think (see *pages 64–69*).

Another way to perk up the bedroom is to introduce color and pattern with a skirted table. Use layered skirts for a generous appear-

BEDROOMS
&BATHS

ance and edge them with piping for a finished look. Arrange a lamp, books, photos, and accessories in a display that reflects your interests.

Fabric can transform bathroom sinks, too, softening hard lines and hiding unsightly pipes. Play up the color scheme with coordinating shower curtain, rug, and hand towels to give the room a fresh new look.

Yards of fabric knotted through decorative towel rings make a lavish frame for the bed. Use anchor bolts to secure the rings to the ceiling, defining a rectangle that's slightly larger than the bed. When measuring for fabric, add 24 inches to the floor-to-ceiling measurement for knotting and puddling. Add 12 to 18 inches to the horizontal swags for draping. Knot each length of fabric to the rings separately, arranging the folds to hide fabric ends.

BOXED VALANCE BED DRAPERIES

The secret to creating this romantic canopy is to hang the curtains on tension rods that are hidden inside the box cornice. Attach the cornice to the ceiling joists with anchor bolts.

INSTRUCTIONS

1 **To make cornice box,** cut two 17¼-inch pieces from 1×6 board for sides. For front, cut 1 piece 2 inches wider than bed (56 inches for double bed). Assemble into 3-sided 18-inch-deep box using glue and finishing nails. Use wood screws and nails to attach wood strips flush with top of box as follows: 1 flush with each open back side (see photo *below right*); 2 fitted into front corners; 2 evenly spaced across front.

2 **Sand, prime, and paint box.** To attach to ceiling, screw through wood strips into ceiling. Fill any gaps between box and ceiling with caulk.

3 **For curtains,** cut 1 toile panel and 1 floral panel for each side and back. Panel width should be 2 to 3 times length of rod they fit and same measurement as floor to ceiling.

4 **Cut check fabric as follows:** 2 side ruffles 15 inches by width of side panels plus ½ inch for side seams; 1 front ruffle 15 inches by width of back panel plus ½ inch for side seams. Stitch narrow hems on all edges.

5 **Place back panels** with right sides facing. Stitch top with ½ inch seam. Start side seams 1 inch from top to leave opening for rod; stitch sides and bottom, leaving opening at bottom for turning. Turn, press, and stitch bottom opening closed. Insert rod through top openings and install at back of cornice box against wall (see photo *below*).

6 **For side panels,** stitch right sides together along sides and bottom. Turn and press. Baste top edges together. Place wrong side of ruffle against floral side of side panel; 1½ inches of ruffle should extend beyond top of side panel. Fold extension over panel, encasing raw edges and creating rod pocket. Sew ruffle to panel 1½ inches from fold. Slide rod through casing and install just below wood mounting strip inside box (see photo *below*).

7 **For front ruffle,** turn under 1½ inches along top; stitch close to raw edge to form casing. Insert tension rod and install inside cornice.

8 **For tiebacks,** cut four 24×7-inch pieces from checked fabric. Stitch pieces together in pairs, right sides facing; leave an opening for turning. Turn, press, and stitch opening closed. Sew small curtain rings to upper corners of each tieback. Wrap tiebacks around curtains and secure to wall with small nail or cup hook.

MATERIALS

1×6 pine board (see instructions for lengths)
Finishing nails
6¾×¾×4-inch wood strips for mounting cornice
Wood screws and nails
Wood glue
Primer
White paint
Hollow-wall anchor bolts or mounting screws
Caulk (optional)
Toile, floral, and check fabrics (see instructions for yardages)
Thread to match fabrics
2 tension rods to fit sides of cornice
2 tension rods to fit front and back of cornice
4 small curtain rings
2 cup hooks (optional)

TOOLS

Table saw or handsaw
Sandpaper
Paintbrushes

SWAGGED CEILING CANOPY

MATERIALS

2 coordinating sheets
Thread to match fabric
2 curtain rods, each 2
inches wider than bed
Finials for rods
Paint to match fabric
4 screw eyes with
matching hooks

TOOLS

Awl
Drill (optional)

Add panache to an ordinary bed with a banner draped over curtain rods attached to the ceiling. Make the banner from purchased sheets, one patterned and one plain with a patterned border. Buy an extra set to dress the bed for a coordinated look.

INSTRUCTIONS

1 **For printed ceiling panel,** cut 1 piece 49 inches long by width of bed plus 1 inch for seams. Cut wall panel same width as ceiling panel; for length, measure from ceiling to floor and add 1 inch for seams. Join short ends to create a long narrow panel.

2 **Cut matching pieces** from solid sheet, positioning patterned hemmed edge at front edge of banner. Join in same manner.

3 **Pin long panels together,** right sides facing. Stitch with ½-inch seams, leaving opening at bottom for turning. Turn, press, and stitch opening closed.

4 **Paint curtain rods and finials.** Insert eye screws in rods. Install hooks in ceiling at wall and 30 inches from wall; space them so rods will be centered over bed. Hang rods on hooks and drape banner over rods. Position seam at ceiling-wall joint and patterned border at front.

QUICK TIE-ON CURTAINS

Use wrought-iron curtain rods to frame a plain bed with breezy fabric panels. Match the panels to the bed skirt, or choose a fabric that will coordinate with a variety of linens.

INSTRUCTIONS

1 **Mount curtain rod and swing rods** to wall according to manufacturer's directions. Hang rods at same height as windows or door frame.

2 **For side panels,** measure distance from swing rod to floor to determine length. For width, add several inches to length of swing rod. Cut two panels from each fabric to these dimensions. Repeat for back panels, but divide the length of the curtain rod in half to determine the width of the back panels.

3 **Cut 24 ties,** 2×16 inches. Fold ties in half lengthwise, right sides facing. Stitch 1 long edge and 1 short edge, using ½-inch seam allowances. Turn and press. Pin 3 ties to top edge of each panel, raw edges aligned, placing ties ½ inch from each long edge and at center. (Pin free ends to fabric panel to prevent catching in seam.) With right sides facing, stitch panels together in pairs, using ½-inch seam allowances; leave opening at bottom for turning. Turn, press, and sew opening closed.

4 **Tie panels to each swing rod** and to wall rod.

DESIGN TIP ■ Contrasting fabrics add visual interest to any canopy design. If you aren't confident of your mixing and matching skills, look for fabrics or bed linens in a range of coordinating patterns.

CORNER CURTAINS WITH VICTORIAN BRACKETS

You don't need a four-poster bed to enjoy the feeling of snug enclosure that curtains provide. Gingerbread brackets like those that trim old-fashioned porches hold these curtains in place.

INSTRUCTIONS

1 **To determine width** of each curtain and lining panel, measure arms of corner bracket and add 1 inch for seam allowance. For length, measure floor to ceiling and add 2 inches. Cut four panels from each fabric to these dimensions. Stitch panels together in pairs, right sides facing, using a ½-inch seam allowance; leave an opening for turning at bottom. Turn, press, and stitch opening closed. Sew loop side of hook-and-loop tape to top inside edge of each panel.

2 **Prime and paint brackets.** To mark ceiling position for each bracket, line up point of plumb bob with floor at corner of bed and mark string's position on ceiling with painters' tape. This is where corner of bracket will be attached. Use plumb bob to mark positions for bracket ends and connect points with tape.

3 **Hold brackets to ceiling** along taped lines. Attach to ceiling with screws or hollow-wall anchors. Paint heads of screws or anchors. Staple hook side of hook-and-loop tape to outside edges of brackets.

4 **Press curtain panels** to ceiling brackets along hook-and-loop taped edges. Panels are 1 inch longer than floor-to-ceiling measurement so they will puddle on floor.

DESIGNTIP ■ This treatment works best on beds without a headboard or footboard. For a more open look, cinch each panel with a bow two-thirds from the ceiling.

MATERIALS

4 Victorian corner brackets (available at home improvement stores or through renovation catalogs)

Sheets or fabric in coordinating patterns (see instructions for yardage)

Thread to match fabric

Hook-and-loop tape

Primer and paint for brackets

Screws or hollow-wall anchors

TOOLS

Paintbrush

Painters' tape

Plumb bob

Drill with screwdriver bit

Staple gun and staples

SKIRTED BEDROOM TABLES

MATERIALS

*Fabrics for underskirt and
  overskirt (see instructions
  to determine yardage)*
Thread to match fabrics
*Purchased or self-made
  piping or tassels*
Charms or costume jewelry
Fabric glue

TOOLS

Push pins and string
Fabric marker

Covering a plywood decorator table
with layered skirts is an inexpensive
way to add color and pattern in the
bedroom. And the long skirt hides a
stash of bedtime reading material.

INSTRUCTIONS

1 **To determine underskirt diameter,** measure from floor to table top,
across table, and down to floor on

opposite side. Add 2 inches for hem.
You will need two widths of fabric
this length. Cut one width in half
lengthwise and stitch one half to each
side of remaining width.

2 **Fold fabric in quarters.** Place push
pin in folded corner (this is skirt's
center). Tie 1 end of string to fabric
marker; tie opposite end to push pin
so string equals half of skirt diameter.

Holding string taut, swing marker from one folded edge to opposite folded edges, drawing an arc. Cut along line, trimming away raw edges.

3 **For hemmed edge** *(above right)*, fold raw edge under ¼ inch, then ¾ inch and topstitch in place.

4 **For piped edge** *(above left)*, fold hem over cording and stitch close to cording. For double piped edge

(above center) sew 1 or 2 rows of piping to right side of skirt with raw edges aligned. Turn under hem and topstitch along piping line.

5 **For overskirt,** cut contrasting fabric to a square of desired size. Pipe edge, using narrower piping than at hem (see *above center*); add a second lacy topper and protect surface with ¼-inch-thick glass. Or turn under a

deep hem and topstitch in place (see *above left*). Embellish with purchased charms or costume jewelry, attaching them with fabric glue. Stitch a tassel to each corner.

DESIGNTIP ■ Use the photos *above* to help you decide the size of overskirt you want. A large square drapes generously, while a smaller kerchief gives a prim, crisp effect.

BATHTUB SWAG

Enhance the feeling of pampered elegance in the bathroom with a fabric swag framing the tub. Here, a tassel-trimmed towel bar holds the swag in place at the sides, but you could use decorative knobs or drapery brackets instead.

INSTRUCTIONS

1 **If not using full width of fabric,** hem all edges by turning under and sewing or fusing with fusible web tape. Sew or glue ball fringe to 1 long edge.

2 **Hang cherub just below ceiling,** centering over tub. Center rod on wall beside tub and install according to manufacturer's instructions. Drape fabric over ends of rod and cherub. Hang tassels over towel rod.

MATERIALS
Enough fabric to drape
  wall along length of tub
Ball fringe in same
  length
Thread to match fabric
  or fabric glue and
  fusible web tape
Plaster cherub or bracket
  for top
Towel rod same length
  as tub and hardware
  for installing
2 plaster or fabric tassels
Picture hook or nail for
  hanging cherub

TOOLS
Hammer
Screwdriver or drill
  with screwdriver bit

FABRIC-SKIRTED SINK COVER-UPS

GENERAL MATERIALS

Fabric or tulle for skirt (see instructions for yardage)

Thread to match fabric

Self-adhesive hook-and-loop tape to fit around sink

Fabric glue

ADDITIONAL MATERIALS FOR 2. SHEER SKIRT

Braid same width or wider than hook-and-loop tape to fit around sink edge

ADDITIONAL MATERIALS FOR 3. OVERLAY SKIRT

2 contrasting fabrics for overlays

Rubber band

3 tassels

Cording with flange edge to fit around sink edge

½ yard matching cording without flange

1. GATHERED FABRIC SKIRT

GENERAL INSTRUCTIONS

1 **To determine skirt depth,** measure from sink edge to floor; add top and bottom hems (see individual instructions). For Gathered and Sheer Skirts, double or triple sink perimeter measurement to determine skirt width. Cut fabric to required dimensions. Hem woven fabric on all edges. For tulle, clean-cut edges.

2 **Adhere hook side** of hook-and-loop tape to sink.

1. GATHERED FABRIC SKIRT

1 **Turn under a 2- to 3-inch-deep hem at top of skirt** and stitch in place. Run gathering stitches along hemline; pull up gathers to fit around sink. Stitch over gathers to hold.

Turn under raw edges at sides and bottom of skirt ¼ inch, then ½ inch, and hem.

2 **Cut bias strip to fit over gathers.** Fold under edges of bias strip and topstitch in place over gathering threads. Sew or glue loop side of hook-and-loop tape on wrong side of fabric along hemline. Press onto sink.

2. SHEER SKIRT

1 **To allow tulle to puddle on floor,** add 4 inches to depth measurement. Gather top edge by hand or machine. Sew braid over gathers. Stitch loop side of hook-and-loop tape to wrong side of tulle, aligned with braid. Press skirt to sink. Tulle may be trimmed even with floor.

2. SHEER SKIRT   3. OVERLAY SKIRT

3. OVERLAY SKIRT

1 **Cut skirt 4 inches longer** than measurement from sink to floor and 1 inch wider than sink perimeter. Make narrow hems on sides and bottom. From contrasting fabrics, cut 6 triangles. Bases of triangles should equal about one-third the sink perimeter; stagger the depths as shown *above right*. Stitch each pair of triangles along diagonal edges with right sides together; leave top edges open. Turn, press, and baste top edges closed.

2 **Place overlays on skirt** with wrong sides of overlays facing right side of skirt and raw edges even. Overlap triangles as shown *above right*. Baste 1 inch from raw edge. Lay flange-edged cording over skirt so cord is 1 inch from edge and flange faces raw edges. Sew through all layers along cording. Turn raw edges to wrong side along stitching.

3 **Sew loop side** of hook-and-loop tape to wrong side of skirt along top edge (just under cording). Do not catch triangles in stitching. Press skirt to sink.

4 **Gather bottom edge of fabric** with rubber band 1 to 2 inches from floor. Tuck raw edges to inside, pushing them up through the rubber band. Wrap cording over the rubber band and sew or glue ends in place.

TECHNIQUE TIP ■ For a no-sew alternative, use low-temperature hot glue or fabric glue to attach braid over gathers or to assemble layers of fabric. The glues are best for skirts you won't need to launder often.

CREATE INSTANT ARCHITECTURE WITH A folding screen. These portable accordianlike walls can partition rooms that serve multiple functions or divide a large space into two smaller, more intimate ones. Screens also hide clutter, transforming a corner into a storage area. And, if you live in an older home or apartment with a water heater in the kitchen or bathroom, a screen provides the perfect disguise.

Because a screen works like a wall—and has the decorative possibilities of a blank canvas—it has a big impact on a room's look. Treat it like a

SCREENS
FOR PRIVACY

work of art for a focal point in an otherwise featureless room (see *pages 78–79*), or design it to blend into the background (see *pages 82–83*).

If you place a folding screen in an area with a lot of traffic, be sure it is stable so children and pets can't knock it over accidentally. See *page 83* for instructions.

Look for wooden screens with removable dowels or tension rods so you can change the fabric panels when you're ready for a new look. Add interest by alternating gathered floral panels with flat striped ones. Measure carefully when cutting fabric; panels must be stretched taut.

RIBBONS AND ROSES FOLDING SCREEN

In a room with no special features, a folding screen like this one provides personality as well as privacy.

INSTRUCTIONS

1 **Paint doors white, covering** all surfaces. Let dry. Wrap muslin over lower two-thirds of each door front, pulling excess fabric to back. Staple to door front along top edge of muslin and along sides and bottom of door. Mark 1-foot increments along sides of door for ribbon placement.

2 **Pin 2-inch-wide ribbon to muslin** at center top edge. Run ribbon from center top to marked point 5 feet up from bottom and pin. Pin second ribbon parallel to first, starting 3 feet from bottom to opposite upper corner of muslin. Repeat to make four diagonal bands in one direction. Repeat for opposite direction. Tuck raw edges under and staple. Also staple ribbons at intersections. Glue roses over intersections.

3 **Make a thin solution of** plaster of paris in wide, shallow disposable pan. Dip letters, dried flowers, and other mementos into solution; let excess drain and place items on waxed paper to dry.

4 **Tear edges of watercolor paper** unevenly. Dip paper in plaster, drain, and roll ends to form scroll. Let dry on waxed paper. Paint with white latex paint to match doors. Use broad-tipped marker to write on scrolls. Glue plaster-dipped items to top one-third of screen.

5 **Cover backs of doors with muslin,** folding under fabric at edges for a neat finish. Join doors with double-acting hinges, inserting screws through fabric along edges.

MATERIALS

3 8-foot-tall hollow core doors
Flat white latex paint
6 double-acting hinges
15 to 20 yards of muslin
50 to 60 yards of 2-inch-wide black satin ribbon
36 off-white silk roses 2 or 3 inches in diameter
Love letters, poetry, old photographs, sheet music, dried flowers, and other mementos
Plaster of paris
Heavy watercolor paper
Broad-tipped marker
White glue

TOOLS

Iron
Staple gun and staples
Paintbrushes
Hot-glue gun and glue sticks

STAMPED AND CRACKLED FLORAL SCREEN

Paint a perennial border of summer-bright flowers on a canvas-paneled screen. Joint compound and foam stamps give the panels the look of fresco and your room the feel of an age-old artist's garden.

INSTRUCTIONS

1 **Cut fabric panels to fit screen openings,** adding hem allowances on sides; add enough for casing at top and bottom plus 2 additional inches in length. Hem sides; sew casings in top and bottom. Excess length will shrink from moisture in joint compound.

2 **Tape panel to work surface.** Apply thin layer of joint compound to entire front of panel except casings. Let joint compound dry completely.

3 **Stamp designs onto newsprint** following manufacturer's directions. To create depth in design, stamp smaller and shorter flowers at bottom of panel as foreground. Work up to mid-height, then taller flowers. When satisfied with design on newsprint, repeat on fabric. Coat blocks with neutral glaze before stamping, then stamp two or more times with same stamp to create variation in color and depth.

4 **When stamped design dries,** place panel painted side up on table. Pull panel over table edge, causing joint compound to crackle. Using soft cloth, rub light coat of stain over panel so it seeps into cracks. Wipe off excess stain. Repeat for remaining panels. Install panels on screen.

MATERIALS

Metal or wooden screen designed for fabric inserts
Cotton canvas to fit screen
1 quart all-purpose joint compound (not patching plaster)
Foam decorator block stamps in floral patterns
Decorator block stamp glazes, including neutral
Newsprint
Maple color wood stain

TOOLS

Artists' tape
3-inch-wide putty knife
Small paintbrushes for glaze and blocks
Soft lint-free cloth

■ SCREENS

Start With Ready-Mades

1

Hollow-core doors or shutters purchased from a home improvement center easily become stylish floor screens that create privacy, hide clutter, or add architecture. Joining the panels with double-acting hinges takes only a few hours; finish with wallpaper, stain, or paint.

1. WALLPAPERED DOOR
INSTRUCTIONS

1 **Sand doors and wipe clean.** Apply 2 coats of primer, sanding lightly between coats.

2 **Cover entire door with main paper** (in this example, solid blue) following manufacturer's directions. Fold corners gift-wrap style and wrap to back. Cut piece exact same size as door and apply to back, covering wrapped edges.

3 **Cover top 8 to 10 inches in same manner** using contrasting paper. Cut border to be used as stripes to fit from bottom of top border to bottom of door. Apply to door with vinyl-to-vinyl adhesive. Add horizontal border to cover joint between top border and stripes.

4 **Set screens on floor in upright position** with right sides facing same direction. Use paint cans, concrete blocks, or other heavy items to keep screens upright. Mark positions of hinges, spacing them evenly. Install 3 hinges on each pair of doors according to package directions, making sure screen sits level. If necessary, plane door bottoms so they are perfectly level.

DESIGNTIP ■ If you can't find a shaped horizontal border, make your own by cutting around shapes in a standard border. Coordinate the positions of the stripes with the horizontal border design as shown *above*.

1. MATERIALS
3 hollow-core doors
4 coordinating wallpaper coverings, including a horizontal border and a narrow border that can be applied as stripes
Primer
Wallpaper adhesive (optional)
Vinyl-to-vinyl adhesive
6 double-acting hinges with hardware

TOOLS
Sandpaper
Tack cloth
Crafts knife
Straightedge or ruler
Awl
Screwdriver or drill with screwdriver bit

2. PLANTATION-STYLE SHUTTERS
INSTRUCTIONS

1 **For interest,** select 3 shutters of varying heights. We used 6-, 6½-, and 7-foot panels. Apply clear polyurethane to the shutters. As the polyurethane dries, periodically move the louvers so they don't dry in one position. When dry, sand lightly.

2 **Set screens on floor in upright position** with right sides facing same direction. Use paint cans, concrete blocks, or other heavy items to keep screens upright. Mark positions of hinges, spacing them evenly. Install 3 hinges per pair of shutters according to package directions, making sure screen sits level. If necessary, plane bottoms so they are perfectly level.

DESIGNTIP ■ Use smaller shutters for a screen to hide a fireplace opening, garbage cans, a recycling bin, or a stash of tools or toys. For stability, use 3 hinges per joint.

2

3

2. MATERIALS

*3 unfinished plantation-
  style shutters*
Clear polyurethane
*6 double-acting hinges
  with hardware*

TOOLS

Paintbrush
Sandpaper
Awl
*Screwdriver or drill
  with screwdriver bit*

3. RAISED-PANEL DOOR
INSTRUCTIONS

1 **Fill any gouges or dents** with wood putty. Sand doors so they are perfectly smooth. Wipe clean.

2 **Prime doors, then paint white.** Sand lightly and wipe with tack cloth. Paint doors red. While paint is still wet, wipe over surface with pad of cheesecloth, leaving enough paint to create a grained look. For interest, keep slightly more paint in recesses around raised panels.

3 **Set screens on floor in upright position,** with right sides facing same direction. Use paint cans, concrete blocks, or other heavy items to keep screens upright. Mark positions of hinges, spacing them evenly. Install 3 hinges on each pair of doors according to package directions, making sure screen sits level. If necessary, plane door bottoms so they are perfectly level.

TECHNIQUE TIP ■ Add more doors or panels to make a wider screen. To keep a wide screen steady, screw 2×4-inch wedges to the bottom of every other panel, alternating the side you attach the wedge to. Plain purchased door stops can also be used to stabilize a screen. To make the braces less obtrusive, paint them to match the doors.

3. MATERIALS

*4 hollow-core doors
  with raised panels*
Primer
White latex paint
Red latex paint
*9 double-acting hinges
  with hardware*
Wood putty

TOOLS

Putty knife
Sandpaper
Tack cloth
Cheesecloth
Paintbrushes
*Screwdriver or drill
  with screwdriver bit*

DETAILS DO COUNT. NEW LAMP SHADES, pillows in fresh fabrics and colors, even hand-crafted picture frames can lift a room's spirits. Flowers, too, revive a room. Whether you gather them from your garden or treat yourself to a bouquet from the corner florist, flowers impart a joyous sense of life.

Think of these decorative details as your canvas for creativity. Coordinate colors and motifs with other projects in this book to give an entire room a makeover, or introduce one or two details for a quick facelift.

DECORATIVE DETAILS

Accessories with a lot of personality, such as a fanciful lamp shade or an intricately detailed pillow, will have more impact if you pair them with more self-effacing partners. For example, mix two or three special pillows with a variety of plain ones, and they will stand out by contrast. Catching—and pleasing—your eye is what decorative details are all about.

Stitch vintage tea towels or fabrics into pillows for the family room or porch. Scout flea markets for table linens. If they're stained, so much the better—you won't mind cutting them up for projects. Note how florals, checks, and stripes live well together when they're linked by color.

WINDOW SEAT CUSHION

MATERIALS

Upholstery foam cut to fit
* window seat area*
Muslin to cover foam
Decorator fabric
Thread to match fabric
Purchased or self-made
* cording, double the*
* perimeter of the cushion*
* plus ½ yard*
Zipper 4 inches shorter than
* 1 long side of cushion*

TOOLS

Serrated knife for cutting
* foam*
Sewing needle or curved
* upholstery needle*

Cushions made with a side strip, called a gusset or a welt, have a firm, boxy shape that's perfect for window seats, garden benches, and wicker settees. If you choose a color-coordinated floral or check for one side, you'll have the option of a quick seasonal change with a flip of the cushion. Look for upholstery foam at fabric stores.

INSTRUCTIONS

1 **Using serrated knife,** cut foam to fit window seat area. Cut 2 pieces of muslin to fit top and bottom of foam exactly, adding ½-inch seam allowances all around and piecing as necessary. For gussets, cut 4 strips to fit sides of foam, adding ½-inch seam allowances all around. Join gussets to fit cushion sides snugly. Join top to gusset section, then join to bottom, leaving open on 1 side. Turn; insert foam. Sew opening closed.

2 **Cut top, bottom, and gusset sections** from decorator fabric as directed for muslin, but make 1 long gusset 1 inch wider for zipper. If desired, cover cord to make piping. Baste piping to right sides of top and bottom, aligning seam allowances.

3 **Cut zipper gusset section in half lengthwise.** Baste halves together on 1 long edge, using a ½-inch seam allowance. Stitch seam for 2 inches at each end of gusset. On wrong side, center zipper over basted seam. On right side, stitch zipper in place and remove basting. Join gusset sections to fit cushion snugly. With right sides facing, stitch top to gusset. Open zipper and stitch bottom to gusset. Turn; insert cushion.

ON THE EDGE
PILLOW DESIGNS

Add panache to sofas and chairs with custom-designed pillows. Fringe, buttons, and ties set these cushions apart.

GENERAL INSTRUCTIONS

1 **Cut 2 fabric squares** to desired size (see Design Tip *below*), adding ½-inch seam allowances. To add edge trimming, align seam line of trim with seam line of pillow front, right sides together and raw edges facing same direction; baste in place. Sew pillow front to pillow back with right sides facing and trimming sandwiched in between, leaving most of 1 side open for inserting pillow form.

2 **Clip corners close to stitching;** turn pillow to right side. Pack small wad of polyester fiberfill into each corner. Slip pillow form into cover. Slip-stitch opening closed.

DESIGN TIP ■ Make the pillow cover 1 to 2 inches smaller than the form for a well-stuffed look. For extra-plump pillows, baste fleece to the front and back fabrics before joining them.

1. WIDE RUFFLE

Use the same fabric for the cover, piping, and ruffle for an understated look. Or, for more definition and color, use solid piping with contrasting fabrics.

> ### 1. MATERIALS
> *Fabric for front, back, ruffle, and*
> * piping (about 1½ yards for*
> * 12-inch pillow)*
> *Thread to match fabric*
> *Cording to fit perimeter*
> *Purchased or self-made pillow form*

INSTRUCTIONS

1 **Cover cording** to make piping. Baste to pillow front.

2 **Cut ruffle strips** twice desired width of ruffle plus 1 inch for seam allowances. (Cut strips either on bias or with grain, piecing to yield a strip 3 times pillow perimeter measurement.) With right sides facing, join short ends of ruffle strip to make a continuous circle. Press in half lengthwise, wrong sides together. Baste raw edges, then gather along seam line. Pull up gathers to fit pillow front, aligning raw edges. Baste to pillow front through piping seam allowances. Finish pillow as directed under General Instructions.

2. PRAIRIE-POINT EDGING

Stitch the triangles in matching fabric; or, to save time, use purchased bands of solid-color "prairie points," available at fabric stores. (Prairie points are used for edging quilts.) Add jingle bells or sea shells for fun.

> ### 2. MATERIALS
> *Fabric for pillow and points (about*
> * ⅝ yard for 12-inch pillow)*
> *Water-erasable fabric marker*
> *Thread to match fabric*
> *Purchased or self-made pillow form*
> *Jingle bells*
> *Narrow ribbon*
> ### TOOLS
> *Cardboard for template*
> *Pencil*
> *Ruler*

INSTRUCTIONS

1 **Cut 4-inch square** from cardboard for point template. Cut 16 squares for 12-inch pillow; adjust number for other sizes. Fold squares in half diagonally, wrong sides together, then fold in half again, aligning raw edges. Triangles will measure about 2¾×2¾×4 inches. Mark ¼-inch seam allowance on 4-inch side (raw edges). Align seam allowances and overlap triangles slightly to form 12-inch band. Baste along seam allowances. Repeat to make 3 more bands. Pin to pillow front along seam lines.

2 **Finish pillow** according to General Instructions. Tack bell and ribbon bow to each point.

3. RAG FRINGE

Making your own fringe is a snap with a rotary cutter. Quilters use this tool to cut strips of fabric quickly and cleanly. If you prefer, cut the fringe with sharp scissors—or use pinking shears for a whimsical touch.

> ### 3. MATERIALS
> *Fabric for pillow and fringe (about*
> * 1¼ yards for 12-inch pillow)*
> *Thread to match fabric*
> *Purchased or self-made pillow form*
> ### TOOLS
> *Rotary cutter and mat*
> *Ruler*

INSTRUCTIONS

1 **Cut** 4 strips 4¾ inches wide and long enough to fit perimeter of pillow; add ½-inch seam allowances (49 inches for 12-inch-square pillow).

1. WIDE RUFFLE

2. PRAIRIE-
POINT EDGING

3. RAG
FRINGE

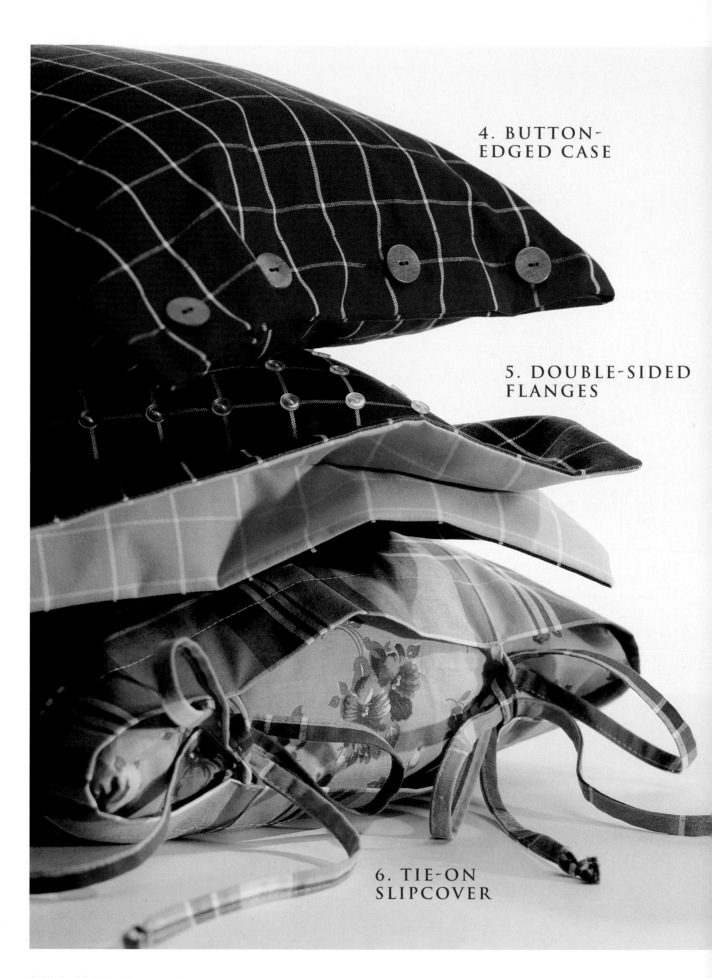

4. BUTTON-
EDGED CASE

5. DOUBLE-SIDED
FLANGES

6. TIE-ON
SLIPCOVER

Layer strips, right side up. Baste along 1 long edge, then stitch through all layers ¾ inch from raw edge.

2 **Using rotary cutter,** cut through all layers from unstitched edge to stitching line at ½-inch intervals. Pin fringe to pillow front, raw edges matching. Assemble pillow according to General Instructions.

4. BUTTON-EDGED CASE

For a quick makeover, slip pillows into tailored, button-down shams. They're easy to make at a fraction of the cost of purchased pillow shams, and you can coordinate them to bedding as well as upholstery.

> ### 4. MATERIALS
> *Fabric for pillow (about ½ yard*
> *for 12-inch pillow)*
> *Thread to match fabric*
> *4 buttons*
> *Purchased or self-made pillow form*

INSTRUCTIONS

1 **Cut pillow front** and back slightly wider and 2 inches longer than pillow. With right sides facing, stitch together on 3 sides. Turn under remaining edge ¼ inch, then 1¾ inches to form hem. Topstitch hem. Turn to right side.

2 **Stitch buttons, evenly spaced,** along inside of bottom hemmed edge. Make corresponding button holes on outside of opposite hemmed edge. Insert pillow and button cover closed.

5. DOUBLE-SIDED FLANGES

Introduce a hint of an accent color with lined, open-flange pillows.

Choose checks in contrasting colors or pair color-matched checks and florals.

> ### 5. MATERIALS
> *Fabric for pillow front and back*
> *(½ yard for 12-inch pillow)*
> *Contrasting fabric for lining*
> *(½ yard for 12-inch pillow)*
> *Zipper to fit pillow back*
> *Thread to match fabric*
> *Buttons for trim (optional)*
> *Purchased or self-made*
> *pillow form*

INSTRUCTIONS

1 **Cut 2 pillow fronts** (1 main fabric, 1 lining) 5 inches larger than pillow form. Cut 2 backs (1 main fabric, 1 lining) 5 inches wider and 5½ inches longer than pillow form. Join pillow front and lining, right sides facing, leaving opening for turning. Turn; slip-stitch opening closed.

2 **Cut back and lining in half.** With right sides facing, stitch each pair of halves together on 3 sides, leaving center edge open. Turn. With right sides of backs facing, baste halves together along center opening. Center zipper on lining side under seam. On right side, stitch all around zipper; stitch basted seams above and below zipper. Remove basting.

3 **Sew buttons to pillow front as desired.** Layer pillow front over pillow back, linings facing. Stitch 2 inches from edges. Insert pillow form through zippered opening.

DESIGNTIP ■ One or two matching pillows will add a subtle touch of color to the sofa or loveseat; for more color, make three to five pillows and reverse the fabrics for the cover and lining. The zippered back

makes it easy to remove the cover for cleaning.

6. TIE-ON SLIPCOVER

Use these tie-on slipcovers to change your existing pillows for the season. Make matching ties from the slipcover fabric, or use narrow grosgrain or satin ribbon to cut sewing time.

> ### 6. MATERIALS
> *Fabric for pillow (about ½ yard*
> *for 12-inch pillow)*
> *Thread to match fabric*
> *Purchased or self-made pillow*
> *covered with decorative fabric*

INSTRUCTIONS

1 **Assemble** slipcover as for Button-Edged Case, but make slightly larger seams so cover fits pillow snugly. Make ties as for Easy-Fit Armchair Slipcover, *page 31.* Tack ties to slipcover edge. Slide slipcover over pillow and tie in place with bows.

DESIGNTIP ■ If your pillows are covered in a floral that seems too heavy for summer, try crisp white cotton; or choose a plaid that picks up one of the main colors in the floral. For winter, give existing pillows more warmth and weight with flannel or chenille slipcovers.

■ PILLOWS

1. LACE MEDALLION

Showcase a piece of new or antique lace (or use a braid medallion) by attaching it to a plain purchased pillow. Nestle a row of matching cording between the pillow and its piped edge for a custom finish.

INSTRUCTIONS

1 **Center medallion on pillow** and blindstitch or glue in place. (If using antique lace, make tiny blind stitches so piece can be removed if desired.) Seal 1 end of cord with fabric glue. Wedge cord along inside edge of piping. Starting at sealed end, glue or sew cord in place around pillow. At end, trim cord to butt with sealed end. Seal with glue; tack or glue in place.

> ### 1. MATERIALS
> *Purchased pillow with*
>   *piped edge*
> *Lace or braid medallion*
> *Narrow cord to fit*
>   *perimeter of pillow*
> *Thread to match lace*
>   *(optional)*
> *Clear-drying fabric glue*

2. TIED AND TASSELED

Top a pillow with a laced cord and tassels, then add a half-dozen buttons as the final touch. Snippets of braid tacked under the buttons hold the whole design together.

INSTRUCTIONS

1 **Cut braid into six 3-inch pieces.** Seal ends of each piece with fabric glue. Fold each piece in half; tack ends of each piece to edge of pillow at corners and midpoint of opposing sides. Let loop ends of braid remain free. Sew buttons over tacked ends.

2 **Lace decorative uphol-stery cord** through loops, crisscrossing pillow. Tie in a bow at one side. Loosen knot of bow and slide one tassel on cord through bow. Tighten knot. Wrap bow tails around tassel cord and trim at top of tassels. Glue or tack to top of tassels.

> ### 2. MATERIALS
> *Purchased pillow*
> *½ yard braid to*
>   *match upholstery cord*
> *Decorative upholstery*
>   *cord (about 3½ yards*
>   *for 18-inch pillow)*
> *Fabric glue*
> *Thread to match braid*
> *6 buttons*
> *2 tassels joined by cord*

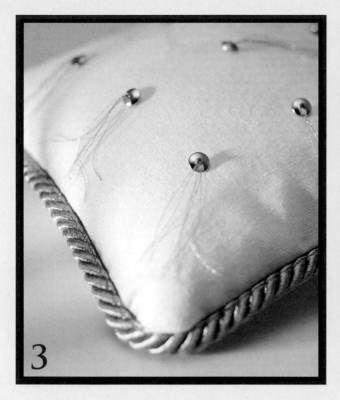

3. BUTTON TRIMMED

Add sparkle to a plain linen pillow with antique beads like the ones shown here; or check the jewelry aisle of crafts stores for similar beads, charms, or buttons.

INSTRUCTIONS

1 **Space beads evenly on pillow** to cover entire surface. Mark placement of each bead with fabric marker.

2 **Thread needle with 3 strands single-ply metallic thread** or 1 strand multiple-ply thread. Insert needle at mark and take 1 small stitch, leaving a 2-inch tail. Stitch again to lock thread in place. Slip needle through bead from back. Knot thread to hold bead in place. Separate plies of multiple-ply thread. Repeat for remaining beads.

3 **Seal cord end with fabric glue.** Slip-stitch cord to pillow edge. Trim and seal remaining end. Slip-stitch ends of cord together.

3. MATERIALS

*Purchased pillow
    with smooth surface
Water-erasable fabric
    marker
Small metallic beads
Single- or multiple-ply
    metallic thread
Matching cord to fit
    perimeter of pillow
Thread to match pillow
Fabric glue*

4. CORD AND TASSEL

Dress up a damask or printed pillow with designer upholstery cord and tassels. For a touch of gold, look for gold-threaded trims in the holiday section of fabric shops and crafts stores.

INSTRUCTIONS

1 **Dip one end of cord in fabric glue to seal.** Slip-stitch cord to edge of pillow. At end, trim cord to fit flush with beginning of cord. Dip in glue to seal. Neatly slip-stitch ends of cord together.

2 **Tack tassel at each corner** behind cord.

TECHNIQUETIP ■ When buying fabric glue, look for products that dry clear, remain flexible when dry, and match the laundry instructions of the fabric you're using. Also check the drying times—they can vary by several hours.

4. MATERIALS

*Purchased pillow
Satin cord to fit
    perimeter of pillow
4 matching tassels
Thread to match pillow
Fabric glue*

EDGINGS FOR SHELVES

Give plain shelves a more finished and decorative appearance with a lace edging or fanciful wood molding. Look for Victorian-style millwork at lumber yards or order it through catalogs that offer vintage-style architectural moldings. Choose trims that are only a couple of inches deep so they don't hide the objects on the shelf below.

INSTRUCTIONS

1 **Glue fringe, fabric lace, or paper lace** to shelf edge with hot glue or clear-drying white glue. To make your own corner shelves, cut ¾-inch plywood into 90-degree triangles. Shelves shown on *page 95, lower left*, have 18-inch sides; adjust lengths to suit your space. For single shelf, cut from 2×6 lumber. For both types of shelves, attach purchased brackets; sand and paint shelves in desired color. Hang with mounting screws.

2 **For decorative moldings,** sand and prime; paint as desired. Paint small wood shapes in contrasting colors; attach to molding with wood glue. Glue molding to underside of shelf, or attach with small L brackets.

Perk up plain painted shelves with edgings of upholstery fringe, fabric lace, or painted millwork embellished with wood cutouts from a crafts store.

DECORATED CHANDELIER SHADES

1. ROSES AND LOVE LETTERS

For a romantic accent in a bedroom or bath, cover a chandelier shade with prints of roses and copies of old letters. Add pressed rose leaves for extra dimension and texture.

1. MATERIALS

Self-adhesive or plain fabric chandelier shade
Photocopies of old letters
Rose-print decoupage paper
Pressed rose leaves
Decoupage medium
Silk embroidery ribbon
Braid or ribbon to fit inside edges of shade (optional)

TOOLS

Tea bag
Foam paintbrushes
High-temperature glue gun and glue sticks or thick white crafts glue
Tapestry needle

INSTRUCTIONS

1 **To age letters,** sponge with damp tea bag and let dry. Tear letters into pieces and adhere to shade, overlapping to cover entire shade. (If using plain shade, adhere paper with decoupage medium.) Trim edges at top and bottom to ½ inch longer than shade and turn to inside, clipping as needed. Glue in place.

2 **Cut out and apply rose images** and pressed rose leaves with decoupage medium. Seal shade with 1 or more coats of decoupage medium.

3 **Thread tapestry needle** with silk embroidery ribbon. Pierce top of shade with needle and weave ribbon around shade. Tie in bow. If desired, trim inside edges of shade with ribbon or braid to cover edges of papers.

2. FAUX LEATHER AND CONE PENDANTS

Brown wrapping paper simulates leather on this little shade. Hemlock cones and eucalyptus "buttons" make fanciful pendants for a rustic feeling; you could also use acorn caps.

2. MATERIALS

Self-adhesive or plain fabric chandelier shade
Brown wrapping paper
Decoupage medium
Raffia
Hemlock, eucalyptus cones, beads
Gold crafts wire
Braid or ribbon to fit inside edges of shade (optional)

TOOLS

Hot-glue gun and glue sticks or thick white crafts glue
Tapestry needle

INSTRUCTIONS

1 **Dampen brown wrapping paper** and crumple it, then spread smooth and let dry. Tear into 2- to 3-inch pieces and adhere to shade, covering entirely. At top and bottom edges, fold paper to inside and secure with decoupage medium or glue. Wrap with raffia, tacking with glue.

2 **To make hemlock pendants,** wrap wire around base of each cone, and twist wire ends. Slip beads onto wire and twist wire ends together. Pierce shade with tapestry needle. Slip wire through hole and twist around itself to secure. If desired, trim inside edges of shade with narrow ribbon or braid.

3. LEOPARD PRINT WITH BEADED FRINGE

Walk on the wild side with an animal print shade that's rimmed in beaded fringe and dried cockscomb.

3. MATERIALS

Self-adhesive or plain fabric chandelier shade
Faux-animal-print paper
Beaded fringe
Dried cockscomb
Braid or ribbon to fit inside edges of shade (optional)

TOOLS

High-temperature glue gun and glue sticks or thick white crafts glue
Tapestry needle

INSTRUCTIONS

1 **Cover shade with paper** as for Pressed Fern Lamp Shade, *page 100.* Glue beaded fringe to lower edge, turning under and overlapping ends. Glue tiny pieces of cockscomb to upper edge. If desired, trim inner edges of shade with ribbon or braid to cover edges of paper.

2. FAUX LEATHER
AND CONE PENDANTS

3. LEOPARD PRINT
WITH BEADED
FRINGE

1. ROSES AND
LOVE LETTERS

SHADE FOR A CANDLE

MATERIALS
*80- or 100-pound
   white paper
Thick white crafts glue
35 to 40 1¼-inch-
   diameter paper
   key tags
Candle follower frame*
TOOLS
Paper punch

BELOW: *Look for candle follower frames at gift and candle stores. They may come with or without metal shades. The cap of the follower sits over the candle, then moves down as the candle burns.*

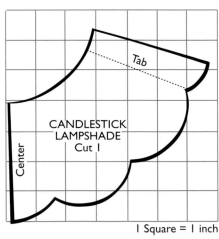

Candles with shades add a festive atmosphere to dinner tables and parties. The key to this project is the brass frame (see photo *at right*), available at gift and candle shops.

INSTRUCTIONS

1 **Enlarge pattern** at *right* to size and cut out. Trace onto white paper, then reverse, aligning center line, and trace to make complete pattern. Fit over frame and mark position of overlap. Punch holes ⅛ inch apart at top and bottom of shade. Glue straight edges of shade together, overlapping first and last holes.

2 **Slip key ring** into each hole at bottom of shade so rings fall in same direction. Place shade over candle follower frame. Keep wick of candle trimmed to ¼ inch or less so flame remains short. Never leave burning candle unattended.

Tab

CANDLESTICK
LAMPSHADE
Cut 1

Center

1 Square = 1 inch

PAINTED LAMP SHADES

MATERIALS
*Purchased paper or
  cloth lamp shades
Blue and green acrylic
  artists' paint in tubes*
TOOLS
*Paper plate
1-inch flat paintbrush*

A pair of old crystal bedroom lamps topped with new shades looks dressy enough to light up the living room. A free-form line of paint adds instant personality to purchased shades.

INSTRUCTIONS

Squeeze blue paint onto paper plate. Dip brush into paint and, using full width of brush, make a loose, uneven wave design around lower edge of shade. Clean brush, then use edge to apply a line of green paint along lower edge of blue, overlapping edges slightly.

TECHNIQUE TIP ■ When painting or trimming the lower edge of a lamp shade, work directly on the lamp. This not only gets your work up to a more comfortable eye level and keeps both hands free, but the shade turns more easily as you work around the edge.

■LAMP SHADES

1. PRESSED FERNS
INSTRUCTIONS

1 **Wrap charcoal paper** around lamp shade, marking top and bottom edges of shade. Add 1 inch all around. Cut out paper. Center shade on paper and glue along top and bottom edges; turn under side edge 1 inch and glue.

Clip excess paper at top and bottom every ¼ inch; turn fringed edges to inside and glue in place. If desired, glue ribbon over fringed edges for a clean finish.

2 **Place ferns on typing paper.** Gently brush backs with matte medium. Pick up each fern with tweezers and place on shade. Lay waxed paper over fern and press (do not rub). Repeat to form ring of ferns around top and bottom. When dry, brush thin layer of matte medium over ferns to seal.

1. MATERIALS
Plain paper lamp shade
80-pound green charcoal paper
Narrow ribbon (optional)
Matte decoupage medium
Pressed ferns
Typing paper
Waxed paper

TOOLS
High-temperature glue gun and glue sticks or white glue
Soft flat ¼-inch paintbrush
Tweezers

2. ROSEBUD GARLAND
INSTRUCTIONS

1 **Wrap fabric around shade** and cut to fit, adding ½ inch all around. Turn under side seam and glue in place. Turn top and bottom edges to inside of shade, clipping as needed, and glue in place. Glue cord to top and bottom edges with flange on inside of shade.

2 **Clip individual rosebuds** and leaves from garland. Glue to top of shade just under cord.

3 **Thin remaining garland** by clipping into small sections and removing excess leaves. Group flowers and leaves into small clusters and wire together. Join clusters with wires so stems are covered but garland is still flexible and can be easily shaped. Fit garland snugly over bottom of shade. If desired, tack in place with glue. Garland may be left loose for easier cleaning.

TECHNIQUETIP ■ Lamp shades that sit close to a bulb may get warm when the light is on. Use glues that are nonflammable and can withstand some heat. Don't use low-temperature glue guns, as the glue may soften.

2. MATERIALS
Plain paper lamp shade
Fabric to cover shade
Flange-edged cord to fit top and bottom of shade
Silk rosebud garland
Floral wire

TOOLS
Hot-glue gun and glue sticks or white glue

3. SEASHELLS
INSTRUCTIONS

1 **Cover shade** with fabric as for Rosebud Garland Shade *(page 100).* Trim inside edges of shade with ribbon.

2 **Practice stamping** on scrap fabric. When stamping on shade, place one hand under stamping area for support. To stamp, dip brush in water. Load with paint, then wipe off excess on paper plate. Brush paint onto stamp. For interest, use 2 or 3 colors per shell, blending with brush. (See manufacturer's instructions for suggestions.) Press stamp onto top edge of lamp shade. Alternate patterns and colors and stamp around entire top edge. For bottom edge, evenly space large stamps in 4 places. Fill in with smaller stamps.

3 **When paint dries,** glue clusters of small shells over stamped shells along shade's bottom edge.

> ### 3. MATERIALS
> *Plain paper lamp shade*
> *Canvas fabric to cover shade*
> *Narrow ribbon to match fabric*
> *Foam decorator block stamps in seashell designs*
> *Decorator block stamp glazes in desired colors*
> *Small seashells*
> *Thick white crafts glue*
> ### TOOLS
> *Flat ¼-inch bristle brush for each glaze*
> *Paper plates*

4. BOWS AND BEADS
INSTRUCTIONS

1 **Cover shade** with fabric as for Rosebud Garland Shade *(page 100).* Trim inside edges of shade with ribbon.

2 **Thread needle** with doubled thread and knot ends. Slide on 1 bead. Loop thread around bead and go through opening again to secure. String beads to about 2 inches. Knot as before, leaving 2-inch tail. Make 3 bead strands for each bow.

3 **Mark placement of bows** on shade, spacing evenly. Twist thread ends of 3 bead strands together. Place dot of hot glue at mark on shade and carefully press threads into glue. Trim thread ends. Tie ribbon into bows and glue over bead strands.

4 **For top trim,** glue 1 end of ribbon at top of shade. Twist ribbon and secure with dot of glue every 3 inches. Turn end under and overlap at beginning.

> ### 4. MATERIALS
> *Plain paper lamp shade*
> *Fabric to cover shade*
> *Ribbon to match fabric (optional)*
> *Small glass beads*
> *Quilting thread to match beads*
> *White glue (optional)*
> *12 inches of 1½-inch-wide sheer ribbon for each bow plus ½ yard for top trim*
> ### TOOLS
> *High-temperature glue gun and glue sticks*
> *Needle for beads*
> *Water-erasable fabric marker*

ETCHED MONOGRAM MIRROR

MATERIALS

Purchased mirror

*Letters for monogram
(from clip art or
embroidery books, or
print out letters of
desired size using a
computer)*

*Clear paper-backed
self-adhesive vinyl*

*Etching cream
(available at crafts
stores)*

TOOLS

Vinegar

Crafts knife

*Glass for cutting
surface*

*Brush to apply etching
cream*

Expand the sense of space and light in a room with mirrors. Group small ones with pictures, or use a larger mirror as a focal point. For added interest, embellish it with an etched monogram (or any traced motif).

INSTRUCTIONS

1 **Trace letters onto paper.** Tape to work surface. Place glass over pattern, and tape vinyl, backing side down, to glass. Trace letters onto vinyl; cut out.

2 **Clean mirror with vinegar.** Peel backing from vinyl and apply to mirror. Apply etching cream, then wash off following manufacturer's directions.

ETCHED GLASS FRAME

Matting takes on a new look when a design is etched directly into the glass. Easy-to-use etching cream and plastic-coated stickers make this project a star when it comes to simplicity.

INSTRUCTIONS

1 **Clean glass with vinegar.** Tape mat to work surface. Center glass over mat and tape down along edges, barely covering glass. Tape off center of glass along inner edges of mat with masking tape. Seal to glass with plastic card. Make sure all edges and corners are straight.

2 **Apply stickers to glass** and seal by rubbing firmly with plastic card. Brush on thick coat of etching cream according to manufacturer's directions; leave cream in place as directed, then wash off, following manufacturer's directions. Dry glass well before inserting into frame.

DOG'S BEST FRIEND FRAME

MATERIALS
Acrylic box frame
Precut mat to fit frame
Bone-shaped dog treats
   in various sizes
Spray polyurethane
   varnish
5-minute epoxy (check
   label for use on
   acrylic surfaces)

Doggone it, pets are people, too. Frame your pooch's portrait in a box adorned with bone-shaped treats. It's simple enough for kids to do. Spray varnish adds durability.

INSTRUCTIONS

1 **Spray all sides of treats** with several coats of polyurethane to seal. Place mat inside frame. Starting with largest treats and working to smallest, glue treats to front and sides of frame.

BUTTON AND TRINKET FRAME

Tiny trinkets, a few inches of plastic pearls, and buttons with interesting shapes are mounded on a plain wooden frame for a look that's vintage—and just plain fun. Paint the frame all one color for a sculptural effect, or leave the elements in their natural forms and colors, if you like.

INSTRUCTIONS

Spread sides and front of frame with sealant. Press buttons, pearls, and trinkets into sealant, adding more sealant as needed. Make sure buttons do not extend so far into the frame that glass will no longer fit. Let dry completely. Spray paint white.

LOW AND LOVELY FLOWERS

MATERIALS

Shallow vase or container
Floral foam
Floral tape
Moss or broad, flat leaves
Assorted flowers ("face"
  flowers such as miniature
  carnations, daisies, or
  roses; spiky "line" flowers
  such as snapdragons or
  delphiniums; and "filler"
  flowers such as baby's
  breath)

TOOLS

Sharp knife

Shallow is good when it comes to centerpieces. Low arrangements don't interfere with conversations by forcing you to peer through a jungle of blooms. Look for containers everywhere—soup bowls, salad bowls, or even coffee cups will do.

INSTRUCTIONS

1 **Soak floral foam thoroughly, then cut** to fit container, allowing foam to extend about 1 inch above container's rim. Secure with floral tape attached at right angles across top of foam. Slip moss or wide leaves (such as tulip leaves) between container and foam. Add water to vase.

2 **Cut stems of face flowers** about 3 inches long. Insert into top of floral foam, starting at center and working toward edges; angle stems so flowers appear to radiate from center. Insert line flowers into sides of foam for horizontal emphasis. Tuck filler flowers into sides among line flowers.

DESIGNTIP ■ Look for floral foam for fresh flowers in crafts stores. It absorbs water; plastic crafting foam and dried-flower floral foam do not.

ARRANGING A CASUAL BOUQUET

MATERIALS

Large watertight container
Floral tape
*Fresh flowers and greenery
(choose a single type of
each, such as mums and
seeded eucalyptus, or
use a mixture)*

TOOLS

Sharp knife (optional)

It's easy to compose a bountiful arrangement that suits an informal style of decorating. The secret is a florist's trick—a grid of floral tape across the mouth of the container. The grid holds flowers loosely in place so the resulting arrangement has a natural grace rather than looking rigidly shaped and controlled. Use this method to turn pitchers, crocks, teapots, or other household containers into vases. If you use a clear glass container, make the grid with clear cellophane tape; it will disappear among the flower stems and leaves.

INSTRUCTIONS

1 **Make a grid across mouth of container** with floral tape as shown *below*. Fill container two-thirds full with water.

2 **Cut flower stems** to 1½ times container's height. Starting in center of container, insert flowers, letting grid support stems. Work outward, trimming stems as necessary so arrangement mounds pleasingly and flower faces appear to radiate from center. Add leaves around outside edges to extend below container's rim. Add water daily.

DECORATOR'S TOOL KIT

TOOL GLOSSARY

Any project is easier to accomplish if you have the right tools. Here are some basic ones to keep on hand.

Awl. An awl, which resembles an ice pick, lets you make a starter hole or pilot hole in wood so nails and screws go in more easily.

Carpenter's level. Don't try to "eyeball" it—make sure your project is level by resting this tool along the top. The bubble will be centered in the vial when the item is hanging properly. An aluminum level doubles as a straightedge for cutting.

Caulk. Choose a paintable acrylic or acrylic combination for indoor surfaces (such as the boxed valance on *page 64*). It's also used for sealing around bathtubs, sinks, and windows.

Clamps. To hold objects together while you work on them or while glue sets, choose multipurpose C-clamps. Use pads when clamping wood to avoid damaging or denting the surface.

Crafts knife. Check crafts stores for retractable single-blade knives and replacement blades. To get a clean cut when cutting thick materials such as mat board or foamcore board, use a new blade.

Electric drill. This tool is indispensable. A ¼- or ⅜-inch drill will handle most home decorating projects. Look for a reversible drill with variable speed control. A screwdriver bit makes quick work of installing valances, shelves, and cornices. Cordless drills are convenient if your project isn't near an electrical outlet.

Glues. Stock up on a variety of adhesives. For gluing fabrics, check crafts and fabric stores for washable fabric glues. For general purpose gluing of porous surfaces such as wood and paper, thick white crafts glue works well. For gluing wood to wood, use carpenters' glue. Five-minute epoxy also is recommended for adhering wood to wood as well as for gluing nonporous surfaces such as metals, glass, porcelain, tile, and plastic.

Grommet tool. This tool, which is sold in fabric stores, is designed to press together the two halves of a grommet, enclosing the fabric between them.

Hammer. Choose a 16-ounce claw hammer for all-purpose jobs. The claw provides leverage for pulling nails.

Handsaw. Quality counts here—an inexpensive saw can chew up your wood and ruin the project. With an 8- to 10-point crosscut saw, you can cut across the grain of the wood, the most common type of sawing. (The points refer to the number of teeth per inch.) A backsaw is a type of crosscut saw with finer teeth (12 to 13 points per inch) for cutting miters. Keep saws covered with a sheath or cardboard when not in use.

Hot-glue gun. Every do-it-yourselfer needs at least one hot-glue gun. High-temperature glue produces the strongest bond and won't soften when exposed to sunlight or heat, but the glue can burn your skin and damage some fabrics and plastics. Low-temperature glues are less likely to burn skin or fabrics, but the glue tends to soften in high-heat areas or in direct sunlight. For greatest versatility, choose a dual-temperature gun that can accept both types of glue sticks; also look for models with built-in safety stands.

Paintbrushes. Choose good quality natural or synthetic bristle brushes for major painting projects. For small jobs or for use with acrylic crafts paints, inexpensive foam paintbrushes work well and are disposable.

Painters' tape. This low-tack masking tape leaves no residue after removal.

Pliers. The two basic types you need to have on hand are slip-joint pliers and needle-nose pliers.

Plumb bob. Look for this tool at a hardware store. It's a cord with a pointed weight at one end; it's used to determine whether a vertical line is straight. To use it, attach the end of the cord to the ceiling and suspend the weight just above the floor.

Tack cloth. Check hardware stores for this loosely woven cloth that has been treated to make it slightly sticky so it picks up sanding dust.

Safety goggles. Always wear goggles when scrubbing with a heavy-duty cleaner, sanding wood, using furniture stripper, or painting the ceiling.

Sandpaper. Keep an assortment of grits (coarse, medium, and fine) on hand for using on raw wood, between coats of paint, or after the final coat of varnish.

Scrapers. Scrapers and putty knives come in different widths for different jobs: removing old paint, wallpaper, varnish, or glue; applying surfacing compound; or removing hard paint. Keep them clean and sharpen them often for most effective use.

Screwdriver. For the best quality, look for cushioned, easy-grip handles and fracture-resistant bars and tips. You'll need both standard and Phillips screwdrivers with tips in a variety of sizes.

Sewing needles and pins. Keep a box of dressmakers' pins, an assortment of sewing needles, and a package of heavy-duty large-eye or tapestry needles on hand. Quilters' pins also are good for upholstery fabrics because they're extra long and have large plastic heads that are easy to see. T pins are heavy, T-shaped pins used for securing fabric temporarily to an upholstered piece.

Staple gun. This is a must for stapling fabric to a chair seat or to a wood strip when making window swags. Look for one that lets you push down at the front where the staple comes out so you'll have extra leverage.

Stud sensor. If you're hanging bed canopies, window boxes, mirrors, or shelves, you'll be glad you have one of these. Electronic versions flash and beep when they locate studs, joists, and other objects, even behind extra-thick walls and floors.

Tape measure. For sewing projects, you'll need a flexible plastic or cloth measure with a metal end. For wood-working projects, a heavy-duty retractable metal tape is helpful when you're working alone; the end of the tape hooks over a door frame, window frame, or the end of a piece of wood so you can measure correctly.

STORING YOUR TOOLS

1 **If the traditional tool box doesn't suit your lifestyle,** look for canvas tool bags at home centers. Or, try adapting a hanging canvas clothes holder or a clear vinyl hanging shoe bag. Small to medium-size tools slip in and out of the cubbyholes or shoe slots and are easy to see. If you buy a plastic one, make sure the plastic is heavy and sturdy so sharp, pointed objects won't pierce it easily.

2 **Stackable plastic bins or trays are other storage options.** If you like to carry your tools with you, use a duffel bag or picnic basket. Small, often-used tools can be kept neatly in a cosmetics bag. Or check hardware stores and discount variety stores for specialty tool organizers that incorporate pockets of various sizes, stackable trays, and a step stool or bucket.

INDEX

Contributors: Suzan Briganti, Mary Mulcahy, Kathy Moore, Peggy Johnston, Jilann Severson, Margaret Sindelar, Maria van Oost, Barb Vaske. **Contributing photographer:** Peter Krumhardt, Bill Rothchild

U.S. UNITS TO METRIC EQUIVALENTS

To Convert From	Multiply By	To Get
Inches	25.4	Millimeters (mm)
Inches	2.54	Centimeters (cm)
Feet	30.48	Centimeters (cm)
Feet	0.3048	Meters (m)

METRIC UNITS TO U.S. EQUIVALENTS

To Convert From	Multiply By	To Get
Millimeters	0.0394	Inches
Centimeters	0.3937	Inches
Centimeters	0.0328	Feet
Meters	3.2808	Feet